An Essential Self

An Essential Self
Ted Hughes and Sylvia Plath

A Memoir

Lucas Myers

·RICHARD HOLLIS·

First published in 2011
by Richard Hollis
an imprint of Five Leaves Publications
PO Box 8786
Nottingham NG1 9AW
info@fiveleaves.co.uk
www.fiveleaves.co.uk

ISBN 978 1 907869 01 3

Designed and typeset by Richard Hollis

Printed by Short Run Press, Exeter

All rights reserved
© Lucas Myers

Five Leaves acknowledges financial support
from Arts Council England

A CIP record for this book
is available from the
British Library

Contents

Preface | 9
Cambridge in the 1950s | 13
Yorkshire | 21
Saint Botolph's Review | 23
Floor Space | 29
The Essential Self | 37
Difficulties of a Bridegroom | 40
In America | 45
The Essential Voice | 48
Olwyn | 55
The Bell Jar | 60
Sylvia and Assia | 63
Devon: Court Green | 69
Accusations | 73
Reputations | 82
Otto and Aurelia | 90
The Ariel Voice | 93
Before Ted | 96
The Fifty-Ninth Bear | 98
The Ego | 101
Myth, Healing and Predation | 104
Ted and Sylvia | 109
Acknowledgements | 113

Lucas, my friend, one
Among those three or four who stay unchanged
Like a separate self...

Ted Hughes
'Visit' – *Birthday Letters*

Preface

Ted Hughes and I met when we were twenty-four and I saw him frequently until we were thirty-nine. After that I saw him much less often, but we corresponded. In the first years, our destinies ran parallel. We married and had two children each, born at about the same time. Then Sylvia Plath committed suicide, I got divorced and the similarities suddenly ceased.

I met Sylvia a little more than a year after I met Ted. When I read her published *Journals* in 2000, I was prepared for the level of the writing by the late poems, but I was less surprised by the intensity of the writing than were some of my contemporaries. What I had to reconcile was the excellence of the writing with the artificiality of the earlier poems and the falseness of her letters to her mother. Talent won out over artifice, but this was not obvious. What surprised me was that Ted had not seen this, nor that the artifice would still be there when what he called her 'Ariel voice' spoke in its true pitch.

The straightforwardness of Ted's other poems contrasted with those in *Birthday Letters*. They were first-rate poems but, because I had known Sylvia, to me they were not convincing. The Sylvia of *Birthday Letters* was not a believable human being. What was believable was Ted's acceptance that someone of her intelligence could be without self-questioning – that she could put one side of her personality under close scrutiny and yet ignore the other side. To question her rationalizations was not possible, 'she can't be helped that way', as Ted put it. I saw Sylvia as abnormal and, gifted though she was, that her gift could only develop as far as it did through the stimulus of Ted. Ted thought – insofar as he considered it – she was more self-sufficient. He did not reckon with her dependence on his stimulus.

Sylvia took exception to Ted's adultery, but she was not driven to suicide by that adultery – otherwise she would not have accepted the infidelities of others to her. Ted was driven to waywardness by Sylvia herself; his subsequent sexual adventures gave hostile critics material for argument, but his behaviour with Sylvia was different from his behaviour in his later life. I believe the threat of divorce in her letters to her mother, to her benefactor, the author Edna Higgins Prouty, and to her Aunt Dot, were intended, by either subconscious or conscious design, to secure financial aid. She was right: the financial aid was indeed forthcoming.

Soon after the birth of their first child, Frieda, Ted was crossing the hump of Chalk Farm Bridge when he came across a man with a fox cub zipped into his jacket. The man offered to sell it and he could have bought it; he thought of buying it; he was tempted to buy it. But in that instant of decision, he did not buy it. The flat at Chalcot Square was extremely small. But – as he fails to say in 'Epiphany' (*Birthday Letters*) – it was Sylvia's reaction that weighed in the decision. He knew what a rage it would put her into, all expressed in terms of care for the baby. The third possibility is not mentioned: keeping it until he could find a suitable home for it or taking it to the country. The fox, the emblem of poetry for Ted, gave way to inconvenience, which Sylvia would have expressed as 'the baby's well-being'. The baby was about one month old. 'Our marriage had failed,' Ted concluded. That was in 1960. Did he already realize it in 1960? Or was this in retrospect? I had gathered a more hopeful but less factual view of the marriage from his letters, which never mentioned anything unfavourable to Sylvia; still, I did not accept Ted's explanation in the poem as factual when I read it – or as anything other than delusional.

For over three years, he never spoke badly of Sylvia to me. But Sylvia could not be helped in the way Ted tried to help her, and I thought she could not be helped in any other way. If she could have been helped, she would no longer have been Sylvia. Whether she could have written other, but different, poems of distinction is a matter for conjecture, but my own guess is that the Ariel voice is the voice of her best verse. Her achievement is in the Ariel voice and it was precipitated by Ted, not by the voices of earlier lovers. It was certainly not precipitated by the voice supplied by her psychiatrist, though that was the voice she hearkened to. She discovered the Ariel voice as a reaction to it, as well as in living with Ted.

How, then, did Ted provoke her best poetry? There were two sides to his thinking. One emerged in his introduction to her stories, the prosaic, matter-of-fact side. 'It seems probable that her real creation was her own image, so that all her writings appear like notes and jottings directing attention towards that central problem – herself. Whether this is right or wrong, with some personalities it simply happens,' Ted wrote.* This was factual. It was prosaic. It was the way things seemed to stand in the day-to-day world unless you could get outside yourself and into other mentalities (as notable writers do).

The other side, the entirely separate side that fell in love with Sylvia and wrote *Birthday Letters*, mythologized Sylvia. What lifted her to fame arose from Ted and, before she met Ted, from her reaction to the world around her – that is, her mother, Smith College, Wellesley, and other influences such as her father. It depended on Sylvia's inability to put herself in another person's shoes, her lack of interest in doing so, and her absolute indifference to being anything other than Sylvia. But she was a woman, she became a mother, and she was drawn outside herself by Ted. In part and for a few years, but not conclusively, it depended on Ted.

When Ted first knew Sylvia, in the spring of 1956, he was taken by her apparent passion for writing. It corresponded to his own need and his own belief. He believed that writing was 'the only excuse'. It was the only valid use of one's time if you wanted to write; I agreed with him in those days. Sylvia passionately wanted to write, at least Ted believed so. And she was sexually passionate. He fell in love with her.

*
Plath, Sylvia. *Johnny Panic and the Bible of Dreams*. New York: Harper & Row, 1978. This passage appears in the US edition, but not in the Introduction to the later British edition (London: Faber, 1979).

Cambridge in the 1950s

'You have to meet Ted Hughes,' James Affleck said. With Neil Morris, he was co-editor of *Chequer*, a Cambridge undergraduate literary magazine, and they had accepted two of Ted's poems and two of mine for the November 1954 issue. But Ted was living in London; he had graduated the previous June and I did not meet him until he visited Cambridge in January 1955. He had not knocked on the doors of the BBC or *The Times*, as many graduates in English did, and was making a poor living washing dishes at the restaurant of the Regent's Park zoo, and grafting plants in a rose garden.

Ted was staying near the British Museum at 18 Rugby Street in a small flat that Rugby School had leased to the father of Daniel Huws, who had given the use of the flat over to his son. Dan was now in his second year at Cambridge and walked the streets with pursed lips, wearing a rusty black jacket and boots fastened with wire, a reticent young man who had four poems in the November issue of *Chequer*. He came up to me in the tea line at the University Library and introduced himself, an unanticipated step for so reserved a person. Not having school friends at the university, I had found myself thrown in with the unsmiling followers of my tutor, the celebrated critic F. R. Leavis. Eventually, I did meet Ted and it turned out that we had, all three, been in military service, he in the Royal Air Force, Dan in the Army, and myself in the United States Navy. We were just beyond the age at which you most commonly establish lifelong friendships, but we became close.

It was Ted's custom to accumulate a certain sum of money and to come up to Cambridge and spend his days at the University Library and his evenings at a public house called the Anchor until he was obliged to go back to London and earn more. After the Christmas and New Year holidays, James Affleck brought him to my room in Downing College. He was over six feet two inches tall, a large man of easy manner and ironic smile, with dark brown hair and eyes, wearing a brown leather greatcoat issued to an uncle in the First World War. James left after a while but Ted and I talked the afternoon away. Originally he had thought of studying medicine but at thirteen or fourteen he borrowed a book of Kipling's verse from the library and at sixteen he decided to be a poet, a decision he never reconsidered. He showed me a poem called 'Money, My Enemy'. It was eight or nine lines long and emotive, but the least accomplished of any of his verse I saw then or later. I liked Ted's verse; the only poem I did not like was 'Song', which he wrote at the age of nineteen and was, by approximately five years, the earliest-written in his first volume, *The Hawk in the Rain*. When he was a student at Cambridge, Ted never published anything under his own name, but just before he graduated he published three or four poems under pseudonyms. Even good friends were not aware of his intention to devote his life to poetry.

Ted had a brother, Gerald, ten years older, who had enlisted in the Royal Air Force. Throughout the war, their mother, Edith, was tormented by worry, but Gerald returned home safe. He moved to Australia, was soon married, and made only rare visits to England. Their sister, Olwyn, was almost two years older than Ted; she went to live in Paris soon after graduating from the University of London, but returned to England in 1963. In World War I, Ted's father, William, known as Willie, was one of seventeen in his regiment to get back when the fighting ended. A paybook in his left shirt pocket had saved him from a piece of shrapnel and a bomb had landed between his legs but failed to explode. He had seen soldiers blown into the air and carried horribly wounded men back to a field hospital. He had seen men die.

That first afternoon, Ted and I discovered a coincidence. In the autumn, I had gone to some lectures by Edmund Leach, the celebrated social anthropologist at Clare College who later became

Master of King's, and decided to get out of the contentious atmosphere of English studies at Cambridge and into his stimulating discipline. My moral tutor was displeased, partly because Downing College had no don in social anthropology, and he would have to go to another college to get Leach as my academic tutor or supervisor, and partly because Downing was losing readers of English literature owing to the habit of Leavis, its famous Fellow, of questioning the adequacy of other, less famous, dons. Eventually, though, my moral tutor granted my request.

At Pembroke four years earlier, Ted had been reading English under Matthew Hodgart, a specialist in ballads and Joyce. He liked Hodgart but English studies at Cambridge were not what he had anticipated. They sucked the life out of reading; they were desiccated and argumentative. He had been trying for days to write a paper on Samuel Johnson, due the next morning, but not even the first sentence would come right. Ted nodded over his desk – it was 2 a.m. He crawled into bed. But there was a rustle at the door where his academic gown hung and something emerged. It was a figure big as a man, but a fox on two legs, scorched as though he had come out of a furnace. He advanced to the desk where Ted had been trying to write about Samuel Johnson and put a bleeding paw on the sheet of foolscap. 'Stop this,' it said, 'You are destroying us.' When the fox lifted a bleeding, human-like hand from the sheet of paper, it left a mark.

Ted got out of bed and went to his desk to look at the foolscap sheet. It had been a dream. In a letter to Keith Sagar, Ted describes that dream and a second that he dreamt the following night.* An erect leopard appeared and pushed him back over his armchair, where he awoke. It was not Johnson he disliked. He liked Johnson but disliked the way English studies were carried on at Cambridge.

So Ted changed his field of study to social anthropology for his final year. He immersed himself in literal translations of folk tales and the adventures of shamans in the intermediate world and avoided the theoretical battles most social anthropologists get into if they follow the discipline for a longer time.

*
Letters of Ted Hughes. London: Faber, 2007, 6 July 1979, p.422

[15]

In 1955 there were ten male students for every female student at Cambridge. Members of our circle had girlfriends at one of the women's colleges, Newnham and Girton, or in London, or at a hospital in town. I never met Liz, a nurse, but Ted described her. He was in her bed one morning when the landlady came in with tea. 'What's that lump down there?' the landlady asked. 'That's Ted,' Liz replied and she was obliged to leave the lodging that same day. On another occasion, Liz and Ted attended a party in a house where there was an unoccupied bedroom. Without considering, they fell into the vacant bed. They were not detected, but afterwards Ted felt a weight of guilt for violating hospitality.

I did know Shirley. She was reading English literature at Newnham College, a serious and attractive young woman, intelligent, reserved and very English, of somewhat above-average height, with light brown hair. Ted's friends thought he would do well to marry her and, before he met Sylvia Plath, I never saw him with any other girl. Shirley figured in 'Fallgrief's Girl-Friends' as the beautiful one. It was among the earliest poems to appear under his name, first in *Saint Botolph's Review*, then in *The Hawk in the Rain*.

Dan introduced me to a circle that gathered on late afternoons at the Anchor. Since Ted had graduated the previous June, most of his old comrades in the group were legendary figures to me, but Dan had been in his first and second years when Ted was at university and had known them all. Ted's close friend at Pembroke, Terence McCaughey, was a regular, and had stayed on at Cambridge for advanced study. He had a light touch, a Protestant from Belfast who knew songs and ballads in Irish and Gaelic as well as English. The following year, the School of Scottish Studies in Edinburgh awarded him a grant to record Gaelic stories and songs.

Fintan O'Connell, a Roman Catholic from Belfast and a serious-minded person, often joined us. Joe Lyde, also from Belfast but a Protestant, was the leader of a jazz band. Joe specialized in insulting people at a late point in the evening (Ted and Dan excepted) and this tendency became stronger as time went on, so that it was quite pronounced when he went on to Tulane University in New Orleans. But Ted liked colourful figures and, although Joe alienated friends and Sylvia did not hide her distaste for him, Ted would go out with him in London after Sylvia's death. Joe was the first of our group to die, reportedly of drink. The trombonist in his jazz band, a couple of years younger than he, was Michael Boddy. Michael was big, twenty-four stone in fact. He had been at Marlborough College, a public school, and was the only one of us who sometimes lapsed into what was known as the 'lah-di-dah' accent.

Philip Hobsbaum, who was at Downing College, edited a poetry magazine called *Delta* (in which Ted and I were published). Some forty years later Philip had an article in the *Glasgow Review* in which he told the story of an escape from being smashed on the head by a wine bottle swung by Colin White. Ted had saved him by catching hold of the bottle. Colin was a Scot, the nephew of Keir Hardie, but had grown up in London. During his national service, he had been an officer in Korea. He once gave me a black eye in an exuberant accident. Philip presented himself in the Glasgow article as a scholarly poet who dressed carefully and was acceptable in any company. Hobsbaum has Ted describe him as 'a good man' in the article, and he became helpful to Ted in London before either of them was well known. Colin moved to Mexico, married a Mayan, saved folk materials from disappearance, and died in 2008. Philip also died in 2008, in Glasgow. A calming influence on the Anchor crowd was John Hoare, a schoolmate of Colin's at Raynes Park School, who was a touch taller than Ted but less substantial.

Harold Bloom, who became a prominent literary critic in the United States, was another regular. Hal and Ted did not like each other, though their dislike was never transparent to those around a table at the Anchor. Ted disliked almost no one in those days but he and Hal were temperamentally incompatible and had fundamentally different ways of judging people. Hal thought genius was rare and only came out in certain well-established cases; he later made the point in his book, *Genius*. Ted thought the creative spirit existed in a great many people and did what he could to bring it to expression. He never spoke ill of Hal but Hal more than once said to me that Ted's poetry was violent, by which he meant that it expressed a taste for violence. I contended that this was a faulty reading of the poetry, which deals with predation, as it routinely occurs in nature, as well as with other themes. Hal, like Leavis, could unfailingly identify lines from poems or bits of prose and their period; he had passed his boyhood and youth in libraries in Brooklyn before coming to Cambridge and subsequently spent a professional lifetime teaching at Yale. Ted, too, was good at the identification game. One of our group quoted a line from George Meredith and everyone seemed stumped. Eventually Ted spoke up. 'That's Meredith,' he said. 'One of his sonnets.' Apart from Hal's reading of Ted's verse, he was good-tempered and in fact liked Dan's poetry.

Three former classmates at St Paul's School in London – Daniel Weissbort, David Ross and Nathaniel Minton – were a few years younger than Ted. David Ross became Dan Huws's roommate for a term at Peterhouse and Dan introduced the three of them to Ted.

By the time I made these friendships, I had tired of the boarding school regulations of college – if you weren't in by 10 p.m., you were fined and a game of climbing over college walls was more or less condoned by the authorities. I looked for a way out, and put a 'wanted' advertisement for a shack or shed in the college newspaper, *Varsity*. I received a note on blue paper in an elegant but beleaguered hand from Mrs Helen Hitchcock, widow of the rector of St Botolph's church. She offered me a chicken coop, a hut behind the high stone walls of St Botolph's Rectory garden, rent-free in exchange for stoking the stove and renewing coke in the Aga cooker morning and evening. I needed the permission of my moral tutor to move out of Downing College, and finally received it.

I swept the chicken coop out. A long time earlier, the hens had departed and I found no droppings on the floorboards, but cobwebs hung under the roof and there was debris in the corners. I painted the walls and brought in a bed, a small desk and a chair, all provided by

Mrs Hitchcock. After the furniture was installed, you could slip in by opening the door seventy degrees, whereupon it jammed against the bedframe. The coop had a long window in the west wall and soon after I moved in, that winter of 1955, the days began to lengthen. As spring came on, the trees and bushes in the garden put out young leaves and before dawn birds began to sing. This was a Garden of Eden.

The first night Ted came up from London after my move, he slept on the floor under the long-legged bed. Since he was the guest, he ought to have slept in the bed and I under it, but he rejected that suggestion out of hand. In those days, we termed it 'floor space' when there was no bed for a visitor, but Ted soon bought a tent and pitched it in the garden beyond my door. Later, he said that his green pullover forever stank of hen droppings. He loved a good story.

We thought Mrs Hitchcock was very old (she was sixty). She sent out a large bundle of sheets to a steam laundry once a week, which came back the next day in another steaming bundle, and she invited me to throw my dirty clothes into the pile – no one would see them and when they came back I could pull them out. We became very fond of her; she had been a great beauty in her New Zealand youth and had married a clergyman from the mother country, one who became a don and the rector of St Botolph's, near Corpus Christi College on the east side of the river. The rectory and its garden were over on the west side. Her husband died young and she wound up a widow with four children and a progressive ailment of the eyes that turned her eyelids blue and caused her constantly to blink. The new rector was an unmarried don and she was allowed to remain in St Botolph's Rectory and rent out its rooms.

Anchor friends began to come to the garden and sometimes to bring beer or a bottle of wine, and they also continued to meet at the pub. Punts were tied up downstream from the Anchor; punting was a way to court girls at Cambridge. One night after the Anchor closed, Ted, Boddy, Dan Huws and others detached a punt tied up in the river, crowded into it, and poled as far as St John's College. St John's owned a number of Chinese geese, and they were browsing on the lawns running down to the river. There had been no preconceived plan to capture a goose but when Boddy saw them, he jumped out of the punt, caught one, and broke its neck on the spot. Ted said that since the goose had been killed, it should be cooked. They took the carcass back to St Botolph's, plucked it, and put it into a pot to boil. For a long time, a terrible smell came out of the kitchen but the goose was too tough to eat.*

---

*
An inaccurate story, based on an account by Michael Boddy, appears in Feinstein, Elaine. *The Life of a Poet*. London: Weidenfeld and Nicolson, 2001

Yorkshire

Ted suggested I go up to Yorkshire and stay with his family, which I did in the spring holiday of 1955. He himself was working in London, so I went alone. Ted was born in Mytholmroyd and moved with his family to Mexborough just before he was eight. When I visited his parents, they had recently bought a house, The Beacon, at Heptonstall Slack just above Hebden Bridge. Ted described Mytholmroyd as a 'paradise', where he followed his older brother Gerald around the moors as his 'retriever' of game, but Mexborough was a mining and industrial town and Gerald took a job as gamekeeper in Devon just before the move, probably to avoid it. When the war began, he enlisted in the RAF. Ted and I rarely talked about these changes – our talk was about the countryside, Yeats and American poets.

    I stayed in Ted's room at The Beacon. There was a bookshelf half way around it and the complete works of Dostoevsky were ranged at one end. Ted's mother had bought the set for him. Edith Hughes was a motherly woman and always made sure I had plenty to eat. She gave me breakfast in the morning and dinner when I came home at night. During the day, I would climb down to the canal or up to the moors. They were strange to me – I was accustomed to wild country in Tennessee and bucolic countryside in Surrey, where my sister lived, but I had never seen the unpopulated and dark upland, overcast, the isolated and irregular and unconfigured moorland that I found around Hebden Bridge.

    One morning, I came down to breakfast and William Hughes, Ted's father, seemed preoccupied. Instead of going to his tobacconist and newsagent's shop, he said, 'I think I'll have a read.' He pulled a chair to the window and stared out. When I came back from the moors, he was still staring out. There had been no reading. Mrs Hughes did not seem surprised. It must have happened from time to time. Ted's father had been athletic, a football player before he went off to war and good enough to be invited to turn professional. But when he returned he became a carpenter. Professional athletes were poorly paid in those days. When in 1937 Edith came into a small inheritance, they bought a shop in Mexborough and the family moved.

Many men from that part of Yorkshire had perished in World War I and Ted's father was loth to talk about it, but sometimes his children persuaded him to and in a letter Ted testifies that Sylvia once persuaded him as well.* Those years, when so many men never returned, appear in Ted's poems, for example in 'Six Young Men' in *The Hawk in the Rain*. Gerald's safe return from World War II spared the family similar loss. His mother, a person of psychic gifts which I did not recognize during her lifetime, must have found the war years trying.

After his service in the RAF, Ted lived in Yorkshire again only briefly. But he remained a Yorkshireman. He merely became more and more familiar with the rest of the world. Ted was a Yorkshire youth who grew into a Cambridge undergraduate, an unwilling American, a Londoner and Devonshire farmer, a European, and a cosmopolitan. The secondary school youth who had learned the first book of the *Aeneid* by heart became the translator of *The Tibetan Book of the Dead*, of János Pilinszky's poems, and of Ovid.

*
Hughes, *Letters*, p.169

Saint Botolph's Review

At Cambridge, David Ross had for some time wanted to edit a literary magazine and the project began to take shape in the spring of 1955. For one thing, his father was a successful stockbroker and a kind and generous person, and, for another, David was an only child.

Ted and I were abroad late one night, but Dan Huws and David, his roommate that spring, lived in Peterhouse and were required to be in by 10 p.m. They were late and set about to climb the fence. One of the porters, retired veterans of imperial wars, saw two figures trying to get a purchase at the crossing place, then dropping back into the shadows outside the fence to avoid detection. Or so they thought, but one of the porters had recognized Dan. With another porter, he went to Dan's room and found a figure in the bed. Dan's hair was black, but on the pillow they saw a trail of long, yellow hair. One of the proctors pulled back the bedclothes to discover a young woman. She was not dressed. Her outfit and underclothes were draped on a chair and her shoes were under the bed.

The young woman had come up to Cambridge from London at the invitation of a Peterhouse student, a friend, so one thought, of Dan and David. He had not reserved a room in town (thrift, thrift) for the visitor. Perhaps he had assumed that Dan was away and the bed would be empty. The porters ushered her out into the night. But she knew the way to St Botolph's Rectory garden and its chicken coop.

Somewhat later, Ted and I made our way home. His tent was pitched in the garden but we pushed the door of the chicken coop open for a little more conversation before going to bed. The bed was occupied; the visitor was lying there, this time in her clothes. I said I would sleep under the bed but she refused this offer. There was plenty of room in Ted's tent and she went out there to sleep. It was unlike Ted to thrust himself on a woman (for one thing, he would not seem to need to) but the next morning she said to me, 'Ted's so big and hot.' She was eighteen or nineteen. It was the only occasion I know of when Ted may have seemed to justify the reputation he was in later years stuck with.

The college authorities called Dan and David and their fellow Peterhouse student the next day. The latter spilled the beans, and my college called me in the day after. He had also given the authorities Ted's name, and Ted was questioned, but he had graduated and so was under university but not college jurisdiction.

Our tutors interviewed us. Helga Kobuszewski, who later married Dan Huws, had recently arrived in the rectory and remembers looking out of an upstairs window and seeing Dan stepping away in a smart pair of trousers I had brought from the United States, then coming back, then Ted stepping out in the same pair of trousers to the Pembroke authorities, and then me. Dan and Ted did not own trousers suitable for an interview.

After the interviews, we had to wait a day or two to hear the dons' decisions. Ted had gone back to London but David and Dan lived in the oldest rooms, polished wood and high ceilings, of the oldest college in Cambridge and, with Daniel Weissbort and his medical-student friend Nathaniel Minton but without the informant, we gathered there. Someone brought two bottles of red wine. We opened them. David said he had made up his mind to establish a literary magazine and get it out during the next term. Except for Ted, the contributors were all on hand; we needed to look no farther. When the magazine eventually appeared, only one contributor was added, Danny Weissbort's older brother, George, a painter in London.

The magazine had to have a name. I once wrote somewhere that St Botolph's Rectory was our 'spiritual home', and that formula has been repeated but is not precisely accurate. None of us was 'spiritual' in the usual sense – far from it. But we had aspirations and St Botolph's Rectory was a place of assembly and good cheer. The term

'Review' we picked up from such publications, then famous, as the *Sewanee Review*, the *Partisan Review* and the *Hudson Review*. So the title, the *Saint Botolph's Review*, emerged and was ironically accepted. As yet, however, there were no submissions.

We were all under threat, and thought of the tutors as pig-headed and unimaginative. The discharge of their professional responsibilities inflamed our mood that spring afternoon. Three sets of college and university officials had decisions to make: the Peterhouse tutors, the Downing tutors, and a separate and discrete body that had to deal with Ted, a graduate who was no longer liable to penalties from Pembroke College. Since medieval times, the University had held authority over a circle within a radius of three miles from Great St Mary's tower. In later years, I learned that some of the tutors had laughed at our adventures; others had not.

We drank the wine while our sentences were being decided and I was moved by the circumstances to composition and stepped out onto the stairs to write six four-line stanzas of tetrameter, which I jotted down on notepaper. It was called 'Knaves Dispatched' and became the first submission to the *Saint Botolph's Review* – carelessly proofread, 'sea-silvered' became 'spa-silvered' in the published version.

The sentences were delivered. Dan was sent down for the rest of the term: four days. David was also sent down for the remainder of the term, but he was diabetic and was going down to London to see his doctor in any case. (He died in 2010.) The two of them were guilty of an offence committed every night at every college, climbing over the wall, but the tutors had to take some action. They took far more severe action with the student who was the cause of the affair, whom they sent down for good and deprived of the prospect of a Cambridge degree. His behaviour was regrettable, but depriving a twenty-year old of a degree for failing to secure lodging for a girl deserved a less absolute penalty. Perhaps the dons wanted to get rid of him for reasons of which we were unaware.

Ted returned to London after the initial interview but before the university committee had decided what his penalty would be. It met and forbade him to come within three miles of Great St Mary's, its area of authority. He ignored the prohibition. If he had not, the *Saint Botolph's Review* might not have appeared, at least not with his poems in it, and he and Sylvia Plath would not have met at the party given to mark its appearance. My own sentence was delivered to me by my moral tutor, the serious-minded Mr Stevenson, a classical historian. I remember the meeting in his office vividly because the black eye Colin White had given me was still plain to see and I had dusted it with flour so sat with my right side – the black eye was the left – facing him. Mr Stevenson announced that I was to move out of the chicken coop and seek other lodging. He thought he was getting me out of St Botolph's Rectory but did not succeed because of Mrs Hitchcock's good-heartedness. When I told her what had happened, she offered me her dining room and I moved in the following autumn. She was offering the room where she kept her best china and tableware to an unthinking young man. At the time, I did not understand her generosity.

In the summer of 1955, Ted had a job in London. Peterhouse awarded Dan a grant to study the Etruscans in Italy, and Dan and I agreed that we would hitch-hike to Italy together. Michael Boddy turned up at our hotel in Paris and said he would like to go with us. Dan travelled alone to Rome and after several weeks there Boddy and I returned by train to England, leaving Dan to complete his research.

Back at Cambridge that autumn, the *Saint Botolph's Review* was to be put together, but when the Christmas holiday came upon us we had only a thin issue. The proofs (which I still possess) came back after Christmas and included two poems by Ted, 'Fallgrief's Girl-Friends' and an untitled poem that began 'When two men meet for the first time...', which was called 'Law in the Country of the Cats' in *The Hawk in the Rain*. Between receipt of the proof copy and the printed final, Ted gave David Ross two more poems, untitled in the *Saint Botolph's Review* and beginning, 'Whenever I am got under my gravestone' and 'If I should touch her she would shriek and weeping', but called 'Soliloquy' and 'Secretary' in *The Hawk in the Rain*.

We thought the publication of the magazine should be marked and decided to have a party. It took place on the upstairs floor of the Cambridge Women's Union in Petty Cury, which had a spacious hall but no piano. Joe Lyde's jazz band was to play and a piano was needed to complement the four or five portable instruments, so we hired one and hauled it up the stairs to the first floor. At the party there must have been two or three hundred people – at least it seemed that way. I arrived with my girlfriend Valerie a little late; Dan Huws and Helga Kobuszewski were already there, hanging around the entrance. The band was playing hot jazz just beyond, set up on a platform by the wall. I was dancing something like the twist that, at my American university, I had called the 'hog-wild jitterbug'. This was a less modest dance than Valerie was accustomed to but she gamely began to dance it with me.

Up the stairs came Sylvia (whom I had not met) with her escort, Hamish Stewart, a Canadian, known for his drinking. Sylvia and Dan got into conversation. Hamish disappeared, at least from my sight. Then Sylvia came over and presented herself – Valerie retreating to a chair by the wall as I recall it – in very red lipstick and red shoes, as Helga remembers. She had committed to memory from the *Review* two of my poems and two of Ted's; she recited mine. I stared at the ceiling and the walls; in Sylvia's account in her journal I was drunk, which was probably true. Valerie, a painter, was alone in the chair and must have been thinking that I had deserted her in favour of a more aggressive compatriot, but Sylvia tired of me and asked where Ted Hughes was. He was at the other end of the hall with Shirley. 'Down there,' I said, and pointed.

Valerie and I went back to St Botolph's Rectory a little before midnight, but the party continued for two or three more hours. The next morning, Ted seemed ill at ease. He had a sizeable wound on his cheek where Sylvia had bitten him and drawn blood. In one version I heard fifty years later, Ted hit Hamish, but I think this is an embellishment since I never saw Ted hit anyone in the course of a long friendship. Furthermore, it was Sylvia who made advances; if Hamish wanted to leave her, he had good reason to. According to Sylvia's journal she went back to Queens' College with Hamish, climbed the fence, and slept with him on the floor; later, in the early morning, he returned her to Newnham.*

Revellers had broken the leaded glass windows set in the walls of the Women's Union. The next day, the police made enquiries and Boddy was chosen as emissary. They accepted his explanation, delivered with perfect elocution, that 'some football yobs' had come in and broken the windows.

I thought that Sylvia's bite was a calculated gesture and that Ted would see it the same way, but he was intrigued. The party had been on the night of 25 February. Ted came up again on 9 March and we went to Whitstead, her hall of residence, after midnight. We threw gravel (clods of earth according to Ted in *Birthday Letters*) at what I thought was Sylvia's window on the second floor. She did not appear. I had misunderstood the directions I had been given. The next night, we threw gravel again and a girl came to the window; once more we had the wrong one.

*
Plath, *Journals*, p.213

Floor Space

Whenever I was in London I stayed with Ted at 18 Rugby Street. On 18 March 1956, Ted wrote to me with a request: 'Invite Sylvia Plath to stop by at the beginning of the spring holiday, free lodging for her and for you.' Ted had never before asked me to do anything for him. By then, I was lodged in a rented room in Barton Road and I invited Sylvia for supper, which I cooked on a gas ring on the floor, and passed on the message. Sylvia had reserved a hotel room in London and the excitement I later discovered in her journals was not detectable. On 23 March 1956, the day the spring vacation began, I was with Boddy and met her at the Lamb in London, near 18 Rugby Street and our 'local' public house. Ted must have been working.

Later that evening, we went over to Rugby Street and banged on the door's iron knocker three times, the signal for the flat on the second floor. Ted leaned out of the window and threw the keys to the street and we went up. It became clear that my presence and Boddy's were not essential and the two of us went off to the Lamb. When it closed, we came back. In time, Ted threw the keys down. I waited in the street while Boddy went up. He soon came down again and we sat on the kerb for forty minutes by my watch, a detail I remember because I thought that was long enough to sit outside in the road. When I eventually rapped on the door, Ted threw down the keys and we went up. Ted and Sylvia did not stay long; they went off to her hotel and got in, I was told, with him under her raincoat – a scene that is hard to visualize. The next morning, Sylvia went to the Continent to spend her vacation there and Ted came back and made breakfast.

Boddy later reported that, the evening before, Sylvia was sitting with her hands on either side of her face, opposite Ted whose knees were touching hers. Boddy thought they took no notice of him. But the reason Sylvia hid her face was not indecipherable: she admonished herself to 'Be chaste' and 'in spite of rumor & M. Boddy, let no one verify this term the flaws of the last!'*

Sylvia went to the Continent to look for Richard Sassoon. I did not know who Sassoon was until much later, but her journals and letters give some sense of him. They suggest that he was one of the two men she cared for deeply enough to marry. A year younger than Sylvia, Sassoon was of the same worldwide family as Siegfried Sassoon, the British poet of World War I, and had been born in Paris. He was a colourful existentialist whose parents were living in North Carolina during the years he was at Yale. About four years before Sylvia met Sassoon, Eddie Cohen of Chicago had initiated a frank exchange of letters with her but that relationship was disembodied. Sylvia did not want to see Cohen in the flesh and was rude when she did. He had borrowed a car, driven it without stopping from Chicago to Smith College in Massachusetts, arrived just as she was preparing to leave for her spring vacation, taken her home to Wellesley, and been left at her door without an invitation to come in. Sylvia's mother was troubled by this breach of hospitality on her daughter's part.

Cohen, at that time, hoped to be a psychologist or psychiatrist and did not break off the correspondence. It dealt with contraception, orgasm, and other intimate and practical matters. In spite of her spurning his physical self so rudely, the exchange must have been worthwhile to him since he continued to correspond with her until she ended it several years later. The various young men from New England whom she evaluated in her journals never stirred deep feelings, although Gordon Lameyer from Wellesley for a time believed he was going to marry her. Later, he changed his mind and decided that she was a schizophrenic. More than one of the young men from New England were subsequently to appear as the originals of Sylvia's satire in *The Bell Jar*. So it was Cohen for common sense and Sassoon and Ted for love.

Readers of Sylvia's complete journals may be puzzled by the passages written on the Continent the fortnight before her return on

*
The Journals of Sylvia Plath 1950-1962. London: Faber, 2000, Appendix 8, p.569

[30]

13 April 1956. Was it Ted she loved or Sassoon? It seemed to be both and it could have been either, but Sassoon was not to be found when she went to Paris to look for him. After graduating from Yale in 1955, he had gone to the Sorbonne and had broken with Sylvia in the United States some time before, but she had met him again when he came to visit an old Yale classmate in Cambridge and had spent her Christmas 1955 holiday with him on a motorcycle trip to the south of France. He had written to her (as far as I know) only once after the Christmas holiday, in early March before she went to Paris in search of him, but had left Paris with no forwarding address. For Sylvia and her biographers, he has been untraceable.

The first half of Sylvia's spring vacation was compounded of disappointment at not finding Sassoon and encounters with European men who attracted her. At the offices of American Express, she unexpectedly ran into Gordon Lameyer, the American with whom she had had an affair, but their attraction had lapsed after they quarreled on a trip to Rome. He encountered her at the American Express offices the next day, 13 April, and bought her a ticket on an airplane back to London. Sylvia had been quite uncertain that Ted took her seriously, but she need not have been: Ted received her at 18 Rugby Street and a more serious affair between them began. In four days, she had to go back to Cambridge, but that was long enough for the most important relationship in their lives to begin. Sassoon no longer occupied her mind.

At that time, Ted was working at Pinewood Studios, reading books that might be made into films, but he told me that no more than one in fifty was worth recommending. His salary must have been at least twice what he had earned as a night watchman, but he liked his work at Pinewood much less than pacing alone with his thoughts through the silent corridors of an industrial warehouse. In the top left drawer of his Pinewood office desk, Ted kept a red, rice-paper Oxford University Press edition of Shakespeare's plays and poems, complete in one volume. When he travelled, he took it with him; at work, he pulled it out surreptitiously and read a scene when the supervisor was not in sight. One day, the supervisor came in suddenly and detected him. 'You're not getting on here very well, are you?' he asked. 'No, I'm not,' Ted said, and cleared out his desk.

Ted showed me his rice-paper Shakespeare and I bought the same edition (now on my desk at hand's reach). About five years later, Sylvia tore up Ted's copy in a fit of jealousy; Assia Wevill subsequently replaced it, and later still Sylvia came upon the inscribed replacement after she and Ted were separated. Forty years later he described the scene in 'The Inscription' (*Birthday Letters*).

Sylvia had already returned to Cambridge from her spring holiday in Europe and London. Ted left London and came up to Cambridge soon after the end of Sylvia's spring vacation and set out his camp bed in my new digs. After being expelled from Barton Road, where I had moved after my moral tutor demanded that I quit St Botolph's Rectory, I had found a comfortable room on two levels in Tenison Road. My desk and bookshelves were by the window in the front and there was a good deal of space behind, more than enough for my bed and a washstand and, further back, a shower. Sylvia's letter to her mother of 26 May has Ted staying with me until he moved to Alexandra House. Although I would not invariably advise taking literally what Sylvia wrote to her mother, this is probably accurate. Ted stayed with me in my digs until I went down in the beginning of June and then he moved to Alexandra House, a little less than a month of nights, as *Birthday Letters* has it. On the top floor of Alexandra House, above the restaurant, he put out a mattress but remained faithful to Sylvia; everything that was not Sylvia was 'blind-spot', he reports in 'Fidelity', in *Birthday Letters*, in spite of the 'lovely girl' who respected his resolution like a sister and a wilder one who did not. The poem also gives the reader a sense of his lovemaking with Sylvia ('... the flesh rips you had inscribed / Across my back ...').

At the time, Australia was offering free passage to immigrants from England and Ted had applied for a ticket. He thought of joining his brother, Gerald, once he was ready to go and the ticket had come through. Members of our group thought of somehow hanging together – we had no practical plan but talked about an island – and we regretted his defection. (Two or three years later, he joined that unrealistic dream before it dissipated in marriages and children.) He was seeing Sylvia every day, all day and part of the evening, and, weeks before I graduated, he abandoned the plan to go to Australia. 'I'm getting too fond of Sylvia,' he told me more than once. I was making arrangements to teach at the Mangold Institute in Spain (which Ted remembered as the 'Mango'), after I graduated and, for a while, Ted thought of coming to Spain while Sylvia was finishing her second and final year at Cambridge.

Sylvia was unlike youthful poets I had known before. The others were mostly rebels, difficult and not admired by their teachers, with long hair and scuffed boots, but the authorities approved of Sylvia and she got good grades and had graduated from Smith *summa cum laude*. I do not know what her contemporaries thought of her at Smith – the conventional ones must have thought more of her than the rebels. Even though the actual character of her gifts escaped the authorities at Smith and were discounted by his friends at Cambridge, Sylvia intrigued Ted. His feelings progressed from the bite on 25 February to physical passion on 23 and 24 March to increasingly profound attachment in April and May 1956.

My desk was at a bay window, with the gate and a stone walkway below. Since my tripos (final examinations) was approaching, I could be found at my desk most nights. After Ted had spent the day and evening with Sylvia, he appeared below my window and whistled 'The Wearing of the Green' and I went down and let him in. He was the most considerate of guests; if I was still studying, he sat on his camp bed and pulled out the red, five-and-a-half-inch-by-eight triplicate notebook he had come upon in the industrial warehouse and 'scribbled'. We called it that: scribbling. He gave Dan Huws and me identical notebooks and told us to fill them with poems. Usually the hour was late and I was ready to stop and hear the stories Sylvia had told him or to discuss writers and our hopes for the future, or hear them in the dark until one of us went to sleep. I woke at a normal hour and usually found Ted sitting on his camp bed, fully dressed, scribbling. Or he might be reading one of the volumes of American poetry I had brought over or acquired in London. In 1947, Eyre & Spottiswoode had published twin selections of the poems of John Crowe Ransom and Allen Tate in red and green covers. Ted was greatly taken by Ransom's poems. Ransom was unique but Ted also liked much in other American poetry and found British postwar poetry dry.

I especially remember two of the stories Sylvia told him. In the summer of 1954, she and three other girls had sublet an apartment near Harvard University. She encountered an older doctoral student on the steps of the Widener Library; she was a virgin then, she said, but had yielded to him. When she did, she began to haemorrhage vaginally. They got her to the hospital, where a doctor stopped the bleeding. Later that summer, the doctoral student passed out of her life. Ted took this account as historical and I did as well. In 1973, her sometime roommate at Smith and in Cambridge, Massachusetts, Nancy Hunter Steiner, published a memoir that gives a more elaborated and more alarming account of this incident, and of others.*

It is possible that Sylvia parted with her virginity before the affair with the doctoral student. A likely account has it happening in the front seat of a car with a young man from Wellesley, a college student she had known since childhood. She does not write about this event in her surviving journals (few women who were not virgins at marriage do), but the journals give full details about boys and men who had interested her.

The second story was an account of her suicide attempt of 24 August 1953, told lightheartedly. It was more serious than it sounded and left a scar on her forehead, usually covered by a fall of blonded hair, which was naturally brown. I was literal-minded in those days and did not ask myself how blond hair later turned another colour. In her suicide attempt of 1953, in the basement of her mother's house, she crawled under the front steps and was saved by spitting up most of the sleeping pills her mother had locked away in her closet and Sylvia had found and taken. Two days later, her grandmother heard a

*
Steiner, Nancy Hunter. *A Closer Look at Ariel: A Memory of Sylvia Plath.* New York: Harper's Magazine Press, 1974; London: Faber, 1974

muffled sound in the basement and called Sylvia's brother, Warren, who moved the firewood Sylvia had stacked and discovered her still-alive body. She had ground the side of her head against the stone foundation; Warren got her to the emergency room of the hospital. Sylvia's novel, *The Bell Jar*, gives a fictionalized account of this part of her life. It struck me that Sylvia did not remark on the concern it had caused. Her mother had notified the newspapers and they had given her disappearance, until she was discovered, wide notice. Actually it did not strike me so far as Sylvia was concerned, since I thought I understood her, but it did strike me that none of her biographers mention it. Her financial supporter, Olive Higgins Prouty, who was in Maine when it happened, saw it in the newspapers.

In April and May of 1956, Ted and Sylvia seemed increasingly happy. They took walks in the surrounding countryside and I sometimes joined them. A common pastime was to construct verses based on a beginning line supplied by one of us. The second would supply the next line and the third would contribute a third and the poem would proceed until it reached a conclusion. This practice was later taken up by Ted and Dan and me and, in the long retrospect of half a century, I wonder if Ted and Dan did not consider it childish, but at the time we pursued it again and again.

In the poem 'Chaucer' (*Birthday Letters*), Ted writes of a walk to Grantchester, an idyllic place a short distance from Cambridge, that he places in 1957 but I remember from 1956. Ted's date may be correct and what I remember may not. Sylvia mounted a stile and declaimed part of the Prologue to the *Canterbury Tales* to a field of cows. The cows, fifteen or twenty of them, gathered around and came closer. They began to seem menacing; they stared up at her; but Ted chased them away.

Whether it happened in 1956 or 1957 – Ted was not concerned with newspaper accuracy. There was a difference between us, partly to do with my American literal-mindedness, partly because he loved dramatic gestures. I saw Sylvia's mounting the stile as a theatrical gesture but he accepted it. He must have liked it.

Towards the end of May, *Varsity*, the student newspaper at Cambridge, published a fashion article by Sylvia with photographs of her in a bathing costume. I thought it was a device by the newspaper editor to trick an enthusiastic American into writing a gushing article and I said so to Ted. He agreed with me and his eyes became hooded, protective, like a parent whose child has been teased in the playground. I remember that moment as the point at which I fully gauged the depth of his affection for her.

The Essential Self

Ted and Sylvia were married on 16 June 1956. He did not tell his parents and did not tell Dan or me. Sylvia's mother had arrived in London three days before the ceremony and was the only member of either family at the wedding. Those who want to understand the relationship of Ted and Sylvia could begin by trying to understand why Sylvia wanted the wedding to be confidential, why Ted did not tell his parents, why he accepted this plan without unravelling Sylvia's motives and discussing them with her, and why Sylvia wanted it this way in the first place. His family was told, awkwardly and by letter, two months later; I was told that autumn, also awkwardly. In any case, I had already got wind of it. I had run into them in Paris five days after the wedding in June 1956 and they were wearing rings, which at first I interpreted as conveniences in hotels (at least as I remember it). For a few days, we wandered around the city and dined at cheap restaurants. Clearly, Ted and Sylvia were very happy. At that time, Jean Cocteau was at the height of his fame. 'I'd like to know what he is doing right now,' Sylvia said. We were standing on the Pont Neuf. 'This very minute?' Ted asked. 'This very minute!' Sylvia replied.

By July 1956, Ted was beginning to realize that Sylvia was a more surprising creature than he had reckoned. What Ted saw and the rest of us did not was camouflaged by her forwardness and her lack of self-criticism, but you would think Ted would have been alert to her contradictions. He missed the obvious (or may have relished it) but picked up the subtle. He did not read her journals until she had died but began to realize that he was dealing with what in later years he described as a 'tomb Egyptian', with himself as the 'the gnat in the ear of the wounded / Elephant' of his own incomprehension.* On 23 July,

*
'Moonwalk',
Hughes, Ted.
Birthday Letters.
London: Faber,
1998

on their honeymoon in Spain, she wrote in her journals something from life, or else her imagination, that could have developed into an exceptional short story. It may have happened, it may not have happened, and it was probably a mixture of the two. Sylvia often used her journals as a practice ground for the fiction she planned to write. A woman lies sleepless by her husband at night; she dresses to go out; she goes out and her husband follows; 'wrongness growing, creeping, choking the house, twining the tables and chairs and poisoning the knives and forks, clouding the drinking water with that lethal taint...'*

. . .

Most American schoolgirls would have given themselves away by self-consciousness at being so American or made a point of not being American in an obvious way. But Sylvia was also Teutonic. Her mother absorbed the moralism of New England. Her mother had Austrian parents, and she married a Prussian. I do not detect an overt Teutonic influence in anything Sylvia wrote, but I remember the dislike of Germans from World War II. It was less pronounced, perhaps, in Massachusetts than in Tennessee, but I am sure that Sylvia felt it.

Letters Home, the collection of Sylvia's letters to her mother, includes a few to her brother Warren, who was two and a half years younger. One of them, dated 18 June 1956, talks specifically about her plans at the time of the wedding. The marriage was to be kept secret and her mother was to announce it later as an engagement. Then, when they got back to Wellesley a year later, there was to be another wedding at the Unitarian Universalist Church with Warren as best man and her uncle giving her away. Wedding gifts should be sent to her mother's house in Wellesley. Newnham and the Fulbright Commission were not to be told. By 15 November 1956, she had given up this plan. She did not find it tolerable to live without her husband.

Towards the end of October 1956, Sylvia looked up the 'Fulbright lists' and discovered that three married women were receiving

* Plath, *Journals*, pp.250-51

Fulbright grants. Ted, who was in London, wrote her warily on 23 October and advised her to say nothing even in letters until they could go into her plans on the coming weekend, when she would come down to the capital.* This was a more careful Ted than the one I knew. The following week, she broke the news to the Fulbright Commission and the Newnham authorities. The Fulbright Commission congratulated her and the authorities at Newnham scolded her for failing to tell them in June, when they could have put another girl in her room, but levied no penalty. Her mother accepted her explanation, as mothers will; in any case, Sylvia had a way of making other people believe what she wanted them to believe.

A far less intelligent man than Ted, even if he were in love, would have wondered whether such inconsistencies should be encouraged, but Ted did not challenge them or, if he did, challenged them so ambiguously that she was able to prevent him from coming to the point. Affection and sexual passion stood in the way – and continued for years to stand in the way – of a pragmatic sense of how to 'help' her. Cohen and Sassoon had either been dismissed or else were out of the way, but Ted believed he could 'help' her by avoiding confrontation with her contradictions. Confrontation was what she needed in the normal course of her development and Cohen and Sassoon promoted it whereas Ted and her mother reinforced Sylvia's evasion of it. The 'essential self' he helped develop in this way was a calamity in human terms and a success in poetic terms.

---

*
Hughes, *Letters*, pp.83ff.

Difficulties of a Bridegroom

'You were our Pandarus,' Ted said. That was years later, long after he had sent me the letter asking me to invite Sylvia to 'free lodgings' on her spring holiday of 1956. I had a habit of teasing him when I first knew him, mocking his large speech, his modulations and gestures, until I abandoned it because Ted did not mock people and so had no defence against mockery. In the ordinary course of things, they would have been better off if he had mocked her. I was a Pandarus who thought that nothing would come of the invitation I had conveyed to Sylvia because they were so different from each other. I was radically mistaken in thinking nothing would come of it, but correct in thinking they had differences.

During six of the six years and eight months of their marriage, Ted and Sylvia were rarely apart. They believed that they were like complementary parts of a larger being and effectively said so, but Sylvia subscribed to this theory less pointedly than Ted.

They were, at least, unified in one specific way: they had in common their determination to put into words what they could bring out of themselves. They did not know, of course, what those words would be and the words turned out to be different from those they expected. For example, he thought that the order of birth affected personality – he was the third of three children; Sylvia the first of two. I doubt that Sylvia reflected on the order of birth. Her struggles, often dealt with in her journals, were struggles for success and mastery, not with her own behaviour. Ted is sometimes described as a 'passive' person and, although this is an inaccurate description of anyone as full of initiatives and ideas as he was, he always allowed people to arrive at their own conclusions and did not supply them himself. Those close to him were often stimulated to expand their thinking, but could not imitate him. His manners and discoveries were too original for imitation.

When they were living apart, she in Cambridge and he in Yorkshire and London, Ted wrote letters which give an idea of their close relationship. They took a flat near Newnham in Eltisley Avenue, and moved in on 15 November 1956. Soon afterwards, Ted found a job as a teacher in a secondary modern school, preparing students for the trades. Towards the end of that month, he wrote a story called 'Snow', published in *Difficulties of a Bridegroom* decades later.* He wrote poetry, drama, translations, reviews, criticism and letters, but little fiction, and his reputation rests on work other than his stories. The stories in this volume, however, give a sense of his thinking and, many of them, of his Yorkshire childhood. One story, though, is set in a polar region and was written about two weeks after he and Sylvia had moved into the Eltisley Avenue flat. That would be more than five months after their marriage.

A man comes to himself in the snow. The airplane he is riding in must have crashed into the whiteness. The other passengers have disappeared; they will have sunk into the snow when he was thrown clear. His memory has gone. He cannot tell whether it happened five months or thirty-four years ago.

The man in the snow trudges over perfectly even distances. He counts his steps. He calculates that in five months he has travelled the distance from Southampton to New York (or Yorkshire to Massachusetts). The light has not changed in five months and he cannot tell whether he is in the Arctic or the Antarctic. When the polar night comes, it will reveal the faultless compass of the stars. And the climate will change.

He does not know what is down under him: the earth perhaps, or a frozen lake. If he tries to dig down to find out, twenty feet or yards, he would be covered in snow before he gets far. He would be finished. The one thing he has is energy and he never needs food.

He has lost his memory but he has a few facts. His strides, for instance; it is by counting them that he has worked out how far he has

*
Difficulties of a Bridegroom.
London: Faber, 1995, pp.41-51.
As a play,
BBC Third
Programme,
17 October 1965

[41]

come. There is the earth, although he has not seen it or felt it. Actually there are two ways of knowing what is real. There is the wind in his face. There is his chair too. He carries a farmhouse chair with him and a harness for it on his back, obtained he does not know how, before his memory failed. The chair is different from the other way of knowing. He sleeps on it. Without it he would sink in snow and would no longer exist. It is palpable, it has characteristics, it lacks one of its nine struts, and one leg has been chewed as if by a puppy. It is like his energy: without it he would not exist. It is like a religious chant – chair, chair, chair – it exists by itself, not at a remove, as an abstraction. The solid chair is on his back. As long as it is there, he will endure.

Both Sylvia and her mother had read 'Snow' and said they liked it. But they did not reckon with the distinction, which the story treats, between two ways of knowing. The direct perception of the chair was inimical to Sylvia's way of thinking. If this fact turned out not to suit her, she could supply different 'facts'. The 'fact' that the earth was down there, although unseen, was an absolute. It suited her and some large fraction of her readership. But it was through effort and living with Ted in the second part of 1956 (not an unseen condition like the supposed earth beneath the snow) that poetic skill – as opposed to poetic craft, which she had already mastered – began to come to her. Her willingness to say explicitly what she was feeling was a reality; she put what Ted called the Ariel voice in her mouth and brought it to expression in succeeding years. This explicitness was something she knew because she felt it, whether people liked it or not. It was like the wind and the chair but unlike the putative and abstract earth that must exist down below her.

You might say that Ted invented new 'facts' too, but the truth was that he began with the chair and the wind – direct perception – and went on to the inner life. Direct perception did not proceed directly to theory. The chair and the wind did not inevitably lead to an idea of the self. They came out of observation, observation for example of the hawk on the limb in 'Hawk Roosting' (*Lupercal*): 'I sit in the top of the wood, my eyes closed / Inaction, no falsifying dream' and 'To produce my foot, my each feather / Now I hold Creation in my foot'.

The chair and wind were irrefutable products of direct experience, but it was uncomfortable to follow their logic further, to its necessary conclusion. It was more comfortable to stop somewhere and take up mythologizing. Sylvia followed the earth as she imagined it, beneath the snow, and she was so vital and Ted so determined to see her the way she wanted to be seen. Before he met Sylvia, he had entered into his own inner life unimpeded. Afterwards he never found or looked hard enough for a way that could help her out of unsupported assumptions. Sylvia did not and probably could not review her own behaviour. If challenged, she became hysterical or enraged or broodingly silent. What her mother did and, in an entirely different way, what Ted did was to reinforce her response under the illusion that they were supporting – and thus 'helping' – her.

Eddie Cohen spoke common sense and Sylvia, after three and a half years, dismissed him. Did she get what she wanted? Yes, partially. What she most wanted, as her journals show both before and after Frieda and Nicholas were born, was fame. It would come to her in the form of literary fame. She was a mother and, like mothers, loved her children. Since she was also a poet, she put her feelings into words in a 'rhetorical' (Joyce Carol Oates's word) way, but she did not love them enough to live for them and reject suicide for their sakes. As a man and husband, Ted was at one time 'derrick-striding' and, after his adultery, 'a little man'. Women and men are sexual, their sexuality expressed in one way or another, but she did not have the capacity to care for someone other than herself and neither Sassoon nor Ted persuaded her to want to. Ted was, as she wrote to her brother Warren, the 'counterpart' of her own self but not for her a person in his own right. Sylvia was gifted, she had great industry, and she developed her gift partly by living with Ted, but she did not proceed to the point of learning to detach herself from herself or wanting to do so.

During the summer of 1958, Sylvia wrote in her journals that she and Ted were 'amazingly compatible'. She also wrote that she enjoyed it when Ted was away for a bit, a bit being two or three hours. For a wife, even one as vital as Sylvia, his presence could be overwhelming. There was a danger of becoming too dependent on him, of being unable to make oneself, and being made by him. Ted gave mutually exclusive suggestions: 'Read ballads for an hour, Shakespeare for an hour, history for an hour, think for an hour and then read nothing in hour-bits but everything straight through'.* On one side, they were 'amazingly compatible', which made her feel fulfilled, and on the other was the danger of being overwhelmed. The predominant feeling, however, was compatibility and this dominated their lives for six years.

*
Plath,
Journals, p.401

In America

I never worked out why Ted did not foresee what he would find in America. In part, it was because he liked American poets, especially John Crowe Ransom, and his 'fox' did not like postwar British poetry. Ransom had devised a personal voice to which he responded and other American poets of the period were much more alive than their British contemporaries, who had not felt, or had declined to feel, Ransom's influence.

Ted and Sylvia had gone over to the United States in June 1957 and stayed there until December 1959. They sent me a Christmas card in 1957 in which Sylvia asked, 'Will you ever come home?' to which Ted had appended, 'She means will we ever get back to Europe?' When he first arrived in America, he did not like it. That was not surprising; what was surprising was that he had married an American who had such exaggeratedly American ways. It is not explicit in her journals, but Sylvia herself was half-immigrant, with a Prussian father, maternal grandparents Austrian-born, and a humourless mother who was a vessel of New England moralism. Sylvia castigated herself for never learning German.

Ted had a distaste for Northampton, where Sylvia taught at Smith College; liked Boston much better; the continent even better, which they crossed in the summer of 1959 in an old automobile borrowed from her brother Warren, east to west by the northern route and west to east by the southern. They liked most of all Yaddo, an 'unbelievably beautiful' artists' colony in Saratoga Springs, New York. Ted wrote me letters in which he made memorable observations, for a while very critical of America: 'Life here dies slowly from fingers & the toes' and 'Sylvia would have been an adoring Smith Sophomore all her life but for this job ... which has very brutally disenchanted her'. More believably, it was living with Ted that disenchanted her. Her mother, a widow who had had to find the means to rear two children, was eager for her daughter to earn a college teacher's salary.

When Ted and Sylvia drove across the continent in the summer of 1959, they returned through Tennessee, where they stopped with my parents. In 1995 Ted granted a rare interview to Drue Heinz for the *Paris Review* and told her that I was 'an exceptionally close friend of mine. Luke was very dark and skinny. He could be incredibly wild. Just what you hoped from Tennessee.'* He and Sylvia had spent several nights in the house where I had grown up and it was not at all what you might have hoped for from Tennessee. It did not come out of the Grand Ole Opry, the subsistence farms back in the mountains of 1959, the country accents, or the Elizabethan fiddle music and creaking front steps. The house had twenty-four rooms, counting the ones in the basement, and about eight thousand books. Nor what you hoped for from Tennessee was Sewanee, which was on the wrong side of history, mixing money, at first mostly from England and the east, with southern reactionary tendencies. It produced little of substance and almost went under during the great depression, but had revived somewhat by the time Ted and Sylvia visited it. So my friendship with Ted was not because I was from Tennessee; it was a matter of temperamental compatibility and my good luck. After Cambridge, my progress became stalemated and Ted's did not.

It was Ted with whom I corresponded; I knew Sylvia less well than I thought. In the summer of 1958, I was living in Paris and my parents organized a family reunion; Ted and Sylvia had just moved to 9 Willow Street in Boston, and I scheduled my flight through that city and stayed with them several days in September. Sylvia was different, a little distant, not as she was before, but Ted and I talked out the few days. It was years before I read Sylvia's journals and I did not entirely understand her reserve at that time. The apartment where they were living was small, even for two. Ted's letters were full of arresting ideas, such as the way he thought best – by a conversation among different

* *Paris Review*, vol.37, no.134, Spring 1995, pp.54-94

imagined creatures (as opposed to ratiocination) – and that in the Middle Ages vision was a common way of thinking, a kind of controlled dreaming awake, which was a gift that nowadays has hidden itself entirely.

During the two and a half years Ted and Sylvia spent in the United States, he wrote several times about carrying out the plan for a community, which had originally been for living on an island, but that prospect was subverted by the oncoming births of Frieda in London and of our daughter Rosamond (Ted's god-daughter), which took me back to the United States.

The Essential Voice

From the end of September until December of her final year and in her last fortnight at the end of January and the beginning of February 1963, Sylvia wrote poems that were to be anthologized more than Ted's. It was when she wrote in the Ariel voice that she expressed herself directly and the result was not what either of them had foreseen. It can be heard in her posthumous volume, *Ariel*, and also in a few poems written earlier, in the story 'Among the Butterflies', and in the journals.*

The breakthrough had begun in October or November of 1959 with 'Poems for a Birthday', especially number 7, 'The Stones'. The poem begins, 'This is the city where men are mended', and ends with 'I shall be good as new.' It was about her suicide attempt of 1953. But she was never as good as new afterwards – or before either, if as good as new means what it means for most people: capable of accommodating to the life we actually have to live. Ted wrote from Yaddo that she was composing in an entirely new style, not systematically and one-step-at-a-time as in the past, but from a whole fabric of human experience. They had found Paul Radin's *African Folktales and Sculpture* on the shelves at Yaddo and they (and I) bought it.** Radin's collection brought together eighty-one tales from sub-Saharan Africa including a Hausa story called 'The City Where Men Are Mended'. But there were no men in the story. It was about a good-hearted mother whose daughter was eaten by hyenas and then brought back to life, and an unsympathetic mother whose daughter was eaten and could not be brought back to life. Radin was a California anthropologist who also wrote *The Autobiography of an American Indian*, a volume Ted and I discovered, admired and bought.***

*
Ariel: Poems by Sylvia Plath. London: Faber, 1965

**
Radin, Paul, ed. *African Folktales and Sculpture,* New York: Pantheon 1966

***
Radin, Paul, ed. *Crashing Thunder: The Autobiography of an American Indian.* New York and London: Appleton and Co., 1926

When I had to review Sylvia's earlier poetry, most of it seemed skilful but artificial and, on the night before I had to turn in my copy assessing her first book, *The Colossus*, I found myself in an uncomfortable position. My review would have to be critical. Knowing how sensitive she was to public reception, I did not expect her to forgive me, but she did, or perhaps did not see the review.

The craft was there but not the realization. Sylvia as she was in life was hardly recognizable in her earlier, self-conscious and literary poetry. Her larger reputation rests in great part on what was composed in two months of 1962, then two weeks of 1963. It spoke in the developed Ariel voice and came out (in the evolved form) of the wound that was caused by her husband's affair with Assia. Friends find Sylvia to be one of the great American poets along with Emily Dickinson and Robert Frost, and not solely for her late poems but also for 'Black Rook in Rainy Weather' (1956), 'Epitaph for Fire and Flower' and 'Sow' (1957), and 'Love Letter' (1960). However, it was the poems of the *annus mirabilis* that secured fame on the scale she aimed for, poems spoken in the pure Ariel voice. The Ariel voice is theatrical in the sense that it belonged to a specific personality and looks at the world from the point of view of that personality. Unlike a play, with a whole cast of various characters, a poem speaks with one voice. But that may enlist only the ego of the reader without the surrounding world.

You might have expected Ted to realize where this was leading but Ted did not allow himself to; he anticipated only the best poetry she could write, not what helped produce it. Ted escaped his ego not so much by getting beyond it, as he sought to do, but by displacing it with Sylvia's ego. Sylvia was not aware of the process that was taking place, or interested in it. Before 1962, she had set out on a road that led to the creation of important poetry but one that left children motherless at two years ten months and thirteen months. For six years, the jealousy she felt for her husband had no basis in his unfaithfulness. Then it did. After Sylvia committed suicide, Ted was not the same person. Nor was he at all the same person after Assia committed suicide.

I returned to London on 13 February 1963, two days after Sylvia died, and took a taxi to Cleveland Street where Ted had been living. He was not there and the landlady could not tell me where to find him. She thought he had gone 'to the country'. I went to see Catharine Huws, Dan's sister, the second of five children in the family, who had moved into 18 Rugby Street when Dan had taken a position at the National Library of Wales. She had read in the *Observer* that Sylvia had died and we went to 23 Fitzroy Road, where Sylvia had been living. Ted opened the door. His Aunt Hilda and her daughter Vicky were there, Aunt Hilda with the children upstairs. Ted thought that Sylvia intended to be found and saved, but that was an anodyne for grief and he later changed his opinion. The writer and critic Al Alvarez, who went with him to the coroner's on 15 February, continued to argue that she had intended to be rescued, although there was no evidence for this comforting supposition. The evening Catharine and I went to Fitzroy Road, Ted and the others there held something like a wake without alcohol. Vicky asked Ted to sing 'Waltzing Matilda' and he sang it.*

The story of the day of Sylvia's death and the days immediately following may not be totally recoverable. I remember Ted's governing concerns: the care of the children; the erroneous idea, later reversed, that Sylvia intended to be rescued; and a fixed determination to avoid saying the things reporters are sent to ferret out. Ted was the widower of a suicide and what happens in a marriage, he said and continued to say, cannot be understood by those outside the marriage. The relationship of Ted and Sylvia was unique and has been misunderstood by outsiders and even by close friends, but that has not prevented writers who never met them from commenting on it. I left London before the coroner's inquest.

According to her biographer Anne Stevenson, in the summer of 1953, when Sylvia was twenty years old, she appeared to her mother 'with purple gashes on her legs. When Aurelia questioned her, she replied, "I just wanted to see if I had the guts!" Then she ... cried passionately, "Oh, Mother, the world is so rotten! I want to die! *Let's die*

---

* There were no bongo drums as claimed twenty-four years later by the tenant of the basement flat, Trevor Thomas. The newspaper in which Thomas's account was published were obliged to retract his story.

together!"* Aurelia Plath went to the family doctor, who prescribed sleeping pills and referred her to a psychiatrist, one who started Sylvia on electroconvulsive therapy and whom she enormously disliked. Yet her Wellesley boyfriend, Gordon Lameyer, reported that he saw her every day before he went off to naval officers' training that summer, and he did not detect a disturbance.

Those who have known suicides find different patterns in their deaths. Some cannot bear the pain of living. Some want to make survivors suffer. Some attempt suicide impulsively and do not try again. Some want to be rescued. Others want to make sure not to be. Suicide seems to be more common among poets than in the general population and more common among female poets than among males.

Years before her death, when Sylvia was not yet eighteen, she wrote in her journal that it was her tragedy to have been born a woman.** The reason it was a tragedy was that being a woman restricted her freedom of action and she wanted experiences of every kind. Some time after her suicide attempt of August 1953, she replaced the common sense of Eddie Cohen with the advice of a new psychiatrist, the Freudian Ruth Barnhouse Beuscher. When Sylvia gave up her pursuit of Richard Sassoon and threw in her lot with Ted, I heard her say on several occasions that she wanted seven children. She said that she and Ted were complementary and at the same time that he was the 'counterpart' of her own self. Sylvia did not confront contradictions except when they forced themselves on her, and she became hysterical or walked out when they did. There were different parts to her nature, but the part that ultimately wrote the poems in the Ariel voice was unified. It spoke in the voice of resentment in late September and October until December 1962 and in the register of nullity in the last week of January and the first week of February 1963.

A few years ago, on the Sylvia website edited from Hebden Bridge in Yorkshire, I saw one posting that read, 'I have always loved Sylvia's work and have always been interested in her life ... less than a year ago I made my own suicide attempt'.*** Another posting read, 'Read her. She's wonderful. ... I know what suicide is like in fact I feel suicidal

* Stevenson, Anne. *Bitter Fame: A Life of Sylvia Plath*, Boston: Houghton Mifflin; London: Penguin, 1989, p.44

** Plath, *Journals*, pp.77 and 97ff.

*** Sylvia Plath Forum, Hebden Bridge, October–December 2001 and January–March 2002

[51]

right now but do not worry for me.' In 1974, N.J.C. Andreasen, a psychiatrist at the University of Iowa College of Medicine, wrote, '... Sylvia Plath seems to have suffered from recurrent endogenous depressions. In her particular case, personal factors were of secondary importance, and the cause of her death was a biological or medical illness, unipolar affective disorder'.* A British psychiatrist, Anthony Storr, described Sylvia as 'manic depressive' and 'disturbed and recurrently depressive'.** He spoke of Ted as 'violent' but supplied no evidence of violence. Others found that Sylvia was a borderline personality, or even that she suffered from an extreme post-menstrual syndrome or had been the victim of childhood abuse. Eddie Cohen, in a letter to the *New York Times Book Review* (8 October 1989) on the appearance of Anne Stevenson's biography, said Sylvia was 'what the psychiatrists refer to as a borderline personality'. He also wrote that, 'I have no idea whether Ted Hughes was indeed as long-suffering and patient as his friends make him out to be, but under the circumstances I find it remarkable that he stood it at all as long as he did.' Actually Ted's reaction was complex and that he stood it all over six years has a complex explanation.

The author and critic Diane Middlebrook wrote, 'Depression killed Sylvia Plath.'*** Rationalization put the arguments that led to suicide into Sylvia's mind. Her mother was an essential co-respondent in the rationalizing process. Quite separately, Ted facilitated it by subscribing to the belief that questioning the process directly would not help her. He also relished the idea that someone should want so much to produce poems. So rationalization killed Sylvia Plath. The rationalization was her own, facilitated by others.

In a letter to Keith Sagar, Ted wrote, 'I accepted her temperament and its apparent needs as a given set of facts, to be tended, humoured, cared for, cured if possible in the long term... I surrendered the chance to change her in other ways than by inward concentrated search for the essential voice of an essential self.'**** This was another way of saying that the overriding objective was to help her reach the Ariel voice – 'the essential voice of an essential self' that

*
Andreasen, N.J.C. in *Journal of the American Medical Association*, Iowa City, vol. 228, no.5, pp.595-99

**
Washington Post Book World, 29 September 1991

***
Middlebrook, Diane. *Her Husband: Hughes and Plath – a marriage.* New York; London: Viking, 2003 p.211

****
Hughes, *Letters*, p.722

wrote poems – although both were surprised by the nature of the Ariel voice. Ted later said that the one thing that she did that disturbed him was making poems out of their 'bad moments'. I see it as the inevitable terminus of the unmodified Ariel voice.

When she was with Ted, she became more than she otherwise was and outsiders did not see that. The Ariel voice was always there and, unless Ted were at hand, she was temperamentally unable to vary it. If she was schizophrenic, it was the voice of schizophrenia. By the 1990s, Ted had come to the belief, as his letters to me show, that she would have been better off if he had not coddled her for so long. On the argument that it was a question of avoiding suicide, Ted should not have coddled her; if it were a question of her winding up by producing the best poetry she was capable of writing, he did the right thing. Her suicide could not have been avoided unless, somehow, she was transformed into a non-Sylvia.

Her psychiatrist, Dr Beuscher, functioned as an enabler by giving her 'permission' to hate her mother. A better treatment would have been to break the pattern of rationalization, and thereby to break the pattern of blaming her problems on others. Aurelia Plath was a conventional woman with a gifted daughter whose motherly unwisdom Sylvia strengthened. After Sylvia's death, Ted continued to encourage this unwisdom but in a different way. Furthermore, for a quarter of a century, he had left Sylvia's mother unconfronted by herself. Aurelia Plath was selling Sylvia's manuscripts and the letters from Frieda and Nick, dutifully composed at Carol's urging when they were children, to the Lilly Library and to Smith.

In 2001, Alex Beam wrote a 'biography' of McLean Hospital in Belmont, Massachusetts, where Sylvia had recovered from the suicide attempt of 1953.* He quotes Dr Beuscher as saying that she saved Sylvia's life for eight years. Beam wrote that Dr Beuscher said, '...there was a heavy air of self-dramatization about Sylvia Plath and Anne Sexton... She spoke sort of disparagingly about these well-to-do poets for whom it was a glamorous exercise to show up in the mental hospital'. This was the hospital where several times Robert Lowell

*
Beam, Alex. *Gracefully Insane: Life and Death Inside America's Premier Mental Hospital.* New York: Public Affairs, 2001

and Anne Sexton were patients. Sylvia and her mother were not well-to-do, however. Her benefactor, Olive Higgins Prouty, paid the bills from McLean, as well as funding Sylvia's scholarship at Smith.

Olwyn

It was 1957 when I first moved to Paris. I had written to Ted and asked how to get in touch with Olwyn, his sister. I was surprised when he replied that he did not at all know how we would get along. I insisted and did get in touch with her, and we got along well for many years. At first, I did not understand why he hesitated.

Olwyn had a lively sense of irony and a striking appearance, amber-brown hair and above-average height, and a quickness of manner. When I first met her, she was uncomplainingly employed at the NATO typing pool before NATO's move to Belgium. She was the confessor – although she does not see it that way – of typists who had gone from England to Paris in the hope of discovering a more interesting way of life, the daughters of vicars or headmasters or proprietors of small businesses. These women were often disappointed but Olwyn, who was cheerful and full of stories, fell in with refugees from Eastern Europe, got out of the typing pool at NATO, and went to work for Martonplay, a theatrical and film agency run by Hungarians. I thought she belonged on the Continent, although the matter-of-factness of Yorkshire was a second best.

For most of the time I knew her in Paris, Olwyn lived in a huge one-room flat on the top floor of 30 rue Garibaldi with János Heller, a Hungarian journalist and writer who had escaped from Budapest before the revolution of 1956. He was a childhood friend of Agnes Vadas, a concert violinist (whom I later married) who carried the violin she had won as a prize across a downed tree over a river to the Austrian side during the uprising. Olwyn introduced Ted to János Csokits, the Hungarian poet with whom he collaborated in the translation of János Pilinszky.

Meanwhile, Olwyn and János argued. 'About what?' I asked. Chairs, letters, a piece of cheese... Ted said she got impatient with everyone she knew and forgot it in three days, but the other parties did not. (He did not mention that he was the only person with whom she never got impatient – and had no cause to.) She came to England briefly after Sylvia died and returned in the autumn partly to help Ted with the children at Court Green. By 1965 she had moved to London. When Assia was alive, she had written to me that Ted's sister was 'lovely'; she got along well with her, then did not, then did. 'Philosophize on that,' Ted wrote.

From time to time, I met Olwyn at the Select or Les Deux Magots or some other café. We were sitting one afternoon in a café and she had in her bag a letter just received from Ted with a copy of 'November' and I read it. Ted was collecting poems which were to be included in *Lupercal* and had sent me 'Hawk Roosting' and 'Sunstroke'.* I wrote that I thought that 'November' and 'Sunstroke' were artificial. What I did not realize and Ted did not know was that I had run into obstacles while Ted was surmounting them in the United States. These and other poems in the prospective volume, his second, *Lupercal*, were not artificial but my capacity to read them had atrophied. The volume was notable. Notable also was Ted's capacity to persevere in spite of wrongheaded criticism that he made the mistake of taking to heart. Ted wrote to Gerald that Sylvia was his best critic and, if this were true, she must have helped him. He asked me several times to send detailed criticism of 'November' and 'Sunstroke' but I never did. He asked me whether to call his second volume 'Lupercal' or 'Lupercalia'. 'Lupercalia,' I said. Fortunately he did not take my advice.

Olwyn was a well-informed astrologer and at one point I thought it was she who had interested him in the subject. This was not so, but they had the same sense of humour and were alike in many ways. It was not an arrangement like Wordsworth's with his sister and she did not relieve him, except a year or two after Sylvia's suicide, of childcare, which for many years was his chief responsibility. She was for a long

*
Hughes, Ted.
Lupercal.
London: Faber,
1960

[56]

time Ted's and Sylvia's posthumous literary agent. Her relationship to Ted was simultaneously beneficial and a burden, and never anything in between. She was absolutely loyal to Ted but it did not help because she was his sister and could be discounted. Olwyn was important in Ted's life but did not simplify it.

In 1959, Ted and Sylvia were making plans to come back to England and I was newly married. For a while, we thought of living in some vaguely defined European utopia. They arrived in time for Christmas in Yorkshire, but pregnancies had led us to rethink our plans and, early in the New Year of 1960, Ted and Sylvia were staying with Dan and Helga Huws at 18 Rugby Street and searching for a London flat. Sylvia went out looking every day; she impressed Helga by her determination despite being seven months pregnant. Near the flat where Bill and Dido Merwin lived, Dido saw a building under renovation. It was in Chalcot Square near Chalk Farm tube station and by 1 March Ted and Sylvia had moved into a flat there.

On the way back to the States I returned to London to gather possessions and say goodbye to friends and to my sister and her family in Surrey. I stayed with Dan and Helga Huws at Rugby Street and went over to see Ted and Sylvia the evening I arrived, 3 March. Frieda would be born on 1 April and my daughter Rosamond on 1 May in New Orleans. Sylvia did not feel like going to a pub with us but Ted and I went out to get some beer.

It was the first time Ted had said anything critical to me about Sylvia. I had seen that Ted worked at a table the Merwins had loaned him on the landing inside the flat and that the table had to be moved to one side when anyone came in or went out. Sylvia, he told me, was in the habit of calling out to him from the dining table and that morning he had decided to do a count. She had called 'Ted' or 'Teddie' one hundred and four times. At the pub, we had drunk pints of beer and were away about forty minutes. When we got back to the flat, Sylvia was angry – she stood by the dining table and stared at us silently. It was abnormal. Her eyes bored through us and were filled with rage. Then she put soup on the table. The bowls were half full. When I read

The Silent Woman thirty-three years later, I recognized Janet Malcolm's choice of a title. Sylvia was eight months pregnant and if she did not want visitors there would have been various ways to say so, but it was Ted's full attention she wanted. Sylvia's jealousy of Ted was for his attention and absorption in her, and could be excited by men as well as by women.

Two days later, Olwyn arrived in London for a vacation from her job in Paris with her colleague Janet Crosbie-Hill, a woman who was easy to get along with. They were staying with Janet's mother and came over to see Ted and Sylvia. I was in the flat when Olwyn and Janet arrived. The mood was sombre. Olwyn was smoking; we sat on the sofa and Olwyn and Sylvia alternately pulled up the window to let the smoke escape and pushed it down to keep out the cold air. The window went up and down without a word. Sylvia did not look at Janet or speak to her.

Since we had not had a good opportunity to talk in London, Olwyn had written to me in Surrey, wondering why I had not warned her about Sylvia. She had seen Sylvia in Heptonstall and I had thought she was as aware of Sylvia's peculiarities as I was. I wrote back giving some sort of explanation (as an American) that was inadequate, and as soon as I sent the letter I knew it was wrong. 'I know the American type of which Sylvia is very representative quite well,' I wrote. 'I had always thought her much better than that until this visit. This type has its own desires for any course of action it chooses... Publicly, and somehow in their own conscious minds, this is all done in some high name such as Poetry, Religion, and the Life of Feeling.' It is not only Americans of that type or any type that do this, but I was trying to find an explanation that was also an apology. Sylvia's behaviour was abnormal and Ted might have tried to make her see that explicitly, in which case her reaction would most likely have been hysterical. Or he could have tried indirectly to make her change, which is what he did and what led to the Ariel voice.

Sylvia's practice was to go out into the night when Ted was in conversation with old friends or teachers. He responded by following her.

After six years, his response was exhausted, the affair with Assia began, and the fullness of the Ariel voice was released. Something very intimate and productive had gone on in those six years that an outsider could not fathom and Ted was outdone by the curiosity of people who had never known Sylvia – or in some cases, like that of Alvarez, by people who had known only some part of her. It was the same pattern that had shown itself at Cambridge: Ted had overlooked her red shoes and red lipstick and exaggerated behaviour in favour of her gift, which others had underestimated. Perhaps he relished this exaggerated expression of human nature. A part of Sylvia was inextricably bound up with the red lipstick and red shoes and exaggerated behaviour, and Ted responded to that. Perhaps he did not recognize his own real interest, perhaps he loved outlandish behaviour; probably it was a mixture of two or more strains in his character, but he submerged his own interest.

The Bell Jar

Sylvia could draw, she could cook, she could type eighty words a minute. Ted, too, could do all these things except typing – he was indifferent at that; Sylvia, on the other hand, offered to type a novel I had written and without my explicit knowledge sent out some of my poems to American magazines. It is hard to imagine how she would have time for that. I was pleased that Sylvia wanted to include a poem of mine in the anthology she edited.* She may have been friendly to me because of Ted, although that did not occur to me at the time. (Assia, too, may have been friendly to me because of Ted.) Sylvia created her own opportunities and almost anyone would have been glad to have the chances in life she created. She was the competent East Coast American of her time. In 1961, when they got to Court Green, their house in Devon, she and Ted painted the chairs and tables white for Frieda, and Sylvia decorated them with red birds and roses and hearts. And she and Ted were both ambitious. Ted wanted to bring poetry into existence and thought poetry had a healing effect. Sylvia wanted to publish poetry and fiction and – if she had got that far – travel writing.

For four months before they moved from Chalcot Square in London to Court Green in Devon, Sylvia crossed Primrose Hill every morning to the flat of Bill and Dido Merwin, who were away, to work on her novel, while Ted took care of Frieda. The Merwin flat overlooked the eastern edge of Primrose Hill and, before they left, Merwin had offered Ted the use of his study. He and Dido wondered how Ted managed to write on the landing at Chalcot Square, although he claimed it was a good place. Sylvia used the study without Merwin's knowledge to write a novel.

---

* Plath, Sylvia, ed. *American Poetry Now*, Critical Quarterly Poetry Supplement no.2, 1961

The novel was *The Bell Jar*.* Sylvia sometimes referred to it as a pot-boiler. It became a bestseller and was better than almost any of her fiction. It told the story of an attempted suicide and a stay in an expensive mental hospital like McLean, with characters modelled on living people. Dr Beuscher and Sylvia herself were the sympathetic characters and Sylvia's mother Aurelia and Mrs Prouty the unsympathetic. Its tone was a variant of Salinger's *The Catcher in the Rye*, but lighter, and it was published in England in 1963 under a pseudonym, Victoria Lucas, so that her mother and Mrs Prouty would not see it. Precautions had to be taken, she wrote to her brother Warren, but she soon overrode the precautions and sent it off to Knopf and Harper & Row. They both rejected it respectfully; sympathetic reviews in England apparently came too late to help or were ignored. Eight years later, Harper & Row brought it out profitably. The book was highly entertaining but, as a work of art, it had a flaw: the heroine, who had made a suicide attempt and spent months in a mental hospital, was the same person at the end as she had been at the beginning.

Olwyn explained the applicable United States copyright law to me: a book published outside the country by a United States national could be issued, without paying royalties, by a United States publishing house after seven years had elapsed. By 1970, seven years had elapsed and Knopf was making plans to publish *The Bell Jar*. The editor at Harper & Row warned Ted that Sylvia's estate was about to lose royalties on the book and Ted wrote to Aurelia that publication in the United States could not be avoided. Knopf graciously withdrew plans for its publication, and the novel appeared, including a letter Aurelia wrote to the publisher.

> *Practically every character in* The Bell Jar *represents someone – often in caricature – whom Sylvia loved; each person had given freely of time, thought, affection, and, in one case,* [Mrs Prouty] *financial help during those agonizing six months of breakdown in 1953 ... as this book stands by itself, it represents the basest ingratitude.*

Aurelia had saved all the letters Sylvia had written to her, which were

*
Plath, Sylvia.
The Bell Jar.
New York:
Harper & Row,
1971; London:
Bantam Books,
1972

addressed to 'Dearest Mother' or 'Dearest of Mothers', and they contradicted the picture of the mother in *The Bell Jar*. Aurelia wanted to publish them and it would have been awkward for Sylvia's estate – that is, Ted – to refuse. He gave permission on behalf of the estate and *Letters Home* came out in 1975 with Aurelia's commentary. She may have been surprised by its effect.

In 1963, when Sylvia died, she had left behind letters from her mother, Mrs Prouty, and Dr Beuscher, all urging her to seek a divorce. Predictably, they exasperated Ted. Sylvia had gone to see a solicitor but had not taken any concrete steps to obtain a divorce. She intimated to her correspondents in America, however, that it was her intention to obtain one, which resulted in the receipt of money from at least two of them, reportedly including the life savings of her aunt. Aurelia's letters to Sylvia, apart from those advising her to divorce Ted, have not (as far as I know) survived. Sylvia is said to have destroyed them in the autumn of 1962.

Sylvia and Assia

I did not spend an enormous amount of time with Sylvia or with Assia Wevill but I thought I knew them well. The person Ted discussed future plans with was Sylvia, but she did not reveal to him everything she had in mind when they first were married, such as a second wedding in the Wellesley Unitarian Universalist Church, with presents to be sent to her mother's house.

When Assia committed suicide, I had recently moved to New York. 'Absolutely and totally my fault', Ted wrote. 'With Sylvia it was my insane decisions, with Assia my insane indecision.' Ted's initial analysis was incomplete. It was also incorrect. After Sylvia died, Assia frequently talked to me about a new life, but Ted took no decisive action. Later, he wrote, 'Assia's death completely dismantled me for a while', and he tried to come to terms with the two suicides and the death of Shura, his four-year-old daughter by Assia who died with her, by means of writing poems about them.

Sylvia's, Ted's and Assia's dispositions created the conditions for the suicides, and the differences among their families, which were stark, accentuated what happened. But you cannot say that the suicides would have been avoided if the three had never met – only that they would not have happened at those particular times and places. Sylvia's mother was mechanically conscientious, the mother of a daughter who had attempted suicide before she went to England and the widow of a man whose younger sister revealed, after Sylvia's suicide, that manic depression had run in the family. Assia's family was Russian Jewish on one side and German Protestant on the other.

Ted's family was unified and close but his parents allowed themselves to be condescended to, possibly in order to remain on good terms with their daughter-in-law and grandchildren, or more probably because they gave Sylvia the benefit of the doubt when anything she did or didn't say seemed hard to comprehend. After Sylvia's death, Assia, the mother of their grandchild Shura, needed Ted's parents' toleration. She was not getting it, and Ted was put in an inextricable position. The disasters that overtook Sylvia, Assia and Ted were products of their personalities and families and places of birth, but not of any one of these alone.

In the summer of 1964, when I lived in the flat Assia shared with her husband, David Wevill, at Belsize Park, I had talked to Assia and I corresponded with her when I moved to Paris. I had told Assia, who had offered me the extra room, 'I am the wrong tenant for you,' and had taken a room elsewhere, but that summer, after a trip to Spain, I moved in. By this time, Assia and David were living like sister and brother. On top of the wardrobe in the comfortable spare room where I lived, a book of poems by Sylvia lay open and face down. I picked it up. It was open at 'Metaphors', a poem about a woman who had eaten a bag full of green apples and had boarded a train there was no getting off.

Assia felt haunted by Sylvia. She told me and others so. It foreshadowed 'The Offers', one of Ted's last poems, written twenty-nine years after Sylvia's death, in which he caught different glimpses of Sylvia as though she were alive. Assia herself would reportedly catch sight of Sylvia in a crowd and Sylvia seemed a constant presence. After the publication of Sylvia's poems in 1965, more and more people cast blame on Assia. Sylvia's voice was absolute and unself-questioning and increasingly people discovered that it reflected their own feelings. The story had to have an anti-heroine as well as a heroine and Assia became the anti-heroine. Ted was the anti-hero.

David Wevill, a Canadian, had been on a ship to England when he met Assia. He fell in love with her. After Cambridge, he went out to teach at the University of Mandalay in Burma. In time, she followed him east. Both of them liked Burma and talked about it a good deal, though they said little of their lives before and after. Nathaniel

Tarn was in Burma at this time, but the festive garden parties in Mandalay he has described were hardly recognizable to David, who lived a more day-to-day life. Finally, David and Assia were married in Rangoon, but it was too late. David had been replaced.

Some have described Assia as 'preternaturally' beautiful but that is not precisely how I saw her. She dressed colourfully and with imagination. Postwar London was drab but their flat was full of life. Assia's delicate paintings of flowers and insects hung on the walls of the living room in small frames. David and Assia and I discussed literature; they were both knowledgeable. Assia was a fairly good poet and David was a very good one – Ted said he would not have minded having written one of David's poems. Visitors came, a Canadian journalist on his way back from India, advertising colleagues from Assia's office, literary types, and her father, Lonya Gutmann, on a visit from Montreal. Assia, like her father, made visitors come alive and brought good stories out of them. Evenings were full of spirited conversation. Dr Gutmann was a Russian Jew, the unobservant son of observant parents, who had grown up in easy circumstances. He was continental and well read, not really at home in stiff and rainy Anglo-Saxonia. He had danced with gypsies on the outskirts of Moscow while in medical school and had become physician to the Bolshoi Ballet – at least he and Assia told me so. He had married a German Protestant nurse who became the mother of Assia and her younger sister, Celia.

From Germany, where Assia was born in 1927, the family fled after Hitler came to power; they escaped storm-troopers by hiding in the baggage of a train, got to Switzerland, then Italy, and finally wound up in Israel. Israel was provincial and it took Dr Gutmann and, separately, his wife and the second daughter a long time after the war to get out, but Assia, who met a British soldier stationed in Palestine, left earlier. At the age of twenty, she married the ex-soldier in London, moved with him from England to Canada, was divorced, married an economist in Victoria and, after studying at the University of British Columbia but not graduating, moved with that husband to Toronto and then to the London School of Economics. Assia then went to Burma to join David Wevill. They might have stayed there for another two-year contract, I thought, but Assia had been dilatory in obtaining a divorce from her second husband and the authorities who made appointments at the University of Mandalay did not find it acceptable to have David living with a woman unmarried – at least that is the way I understood it. Assia was very fond of David and once asked me whether you could love two people at the same time. I could give no workable answer to that. Ultimately, she made a choice and became pregnant with Ted's child.

By the time I met David and Assia, they had been together eight years, but the affair with Ted, and Sylvia's suicide, had taken place something more than a year earlier. David was sleeping on the sofa in the living room at least part of the time, Assia in the bedroom. David had left the advertising agency where he had once worked, grown thin, and was reading stacks of books for a publisher at unsatisfactory pay. He set up a desk for me from drawers with a broad writing surface laid out on top; the idea for this, Assia speculated, may have come as a transmission from her, based on the desk made of elm planks and rain barrels that Ted had set up for me on the top floor of Court Green. Or it may have been spontaneous, she thought, since David and Ted were so alike and had ideas in common. I did not find them at all alike although I valued my friendship with each of them. The times were fluid. None of us knew what the future would bring.

Eilat Negev and Yehuda Koren's biography of Assia contains a farewell letter to her father.* Unlike much of the book, it rings true. Dr Gutmann died a few months after Assia. She wrote, 'I have lived on the dream of living with Ted – and this has gone kaput. The reasons are immaterial. There could never be another man. Never.' She asks her father to believe that she has 'done the right thing'. Towards the end of the letter she says, 'Please do not think that I am insane, or that I have done this in a moment of insanity. It was simple accountancy. And I could not leave little Shuri by herself. She's too old to be adopted.' Actually Shura would not have been alone. It was Assia's despair at establishing a home with Ted that made her think she would.

* Koren, Yehuda and Negev, Eilat. *Lover of Unreason: Assia Wevill, Sylvia Plath's Rival and Ted Hughes's Doomed Love.* London: Robson; Cambridge, MA: Da Capo, 2006

Destiny had washed Assia up on an inhospitable shore. She was suited to hold a salon on the Continent but was a refugee in England and Canada. 'After forty, I'll end it,' Ted had Assia say in one of the *Capriccio* poems.* Contradictorily, he said her death was unnecessary, as opposed to Sylvia's. After he had had time to consider it, he saw Sylvia's suicide as unavoidable. When he wrote to me that Sylvia died because of his 'insane decisions' and Assia because of his 'insane indecision', he was struggling with the reasons for their suicides. 'Why did not somebody tell me?', he asked me in the early 1990s. He had allowed himself to be held hostage. Ted misunderstood his error. It was not a positive error. It was the inadvertent error of encouraging Sylvia's narcissism by his vitality when he was at hand, and she lapsed back into narcissism when he was away.

Assia was sociable and generous; she needed friends and was not a solitary creature. When she talked to me about Ted, I could make no suggestions, although I tried to think of some. I never heard her talk about killing herself but, according to Negev and Koren, she spoke of it to others. Just before her suicide on 23 March 1969, she and Ted had taken a house-hunting trip together and found one they liked on Tyneside but they made no decision. The house was grand but Tyneside was not a suitable place for Assia. For Ted, the proposition was not well thought out. What he needed was a mother or mother figure for his children; that much was clear. His parents had moved back to Yorkshire a few months before, but his mother needed care, more than his father was able to give. Ted's sister Olwyn had been living in London for several years. He could not have known that his mother would die a little more than two months after Assia's suicide. The final complication was Assia's discouragement and despair in the months before her suicide.

On 96th Street and Riverside Drive in New York I ran into a friend before I received Ted's letter. (We hardly used the telephone in those days.) He gave me the news of Assia's death. That she had taken Shura with her set me back. Later, David Wevill explained it in the same terms he had used with her father: in Japan, it is a greater sin to

---

* Hughes, Ted. *Capriccio*, engravings by Leonard Baskin, Northampton, MA: Gehenna Press, 1990

leave a child to uncertain care than to take it with you. The concept is called *oyako shinju*.

I think David's feelings for Assia were such that he accepted humiliation in the hope that she would come back to him and they could reestablish their marriage. It was never reestablished. Years later, he passed through New York and stayed a few days with me on the way to the University of Texas at Austin, where he remained. The last communication he received from Assia was a postcard, in Texas, saying that he deserved a happy life.

Devon: Court Green

After Sylvia died, thinking he might live in Yorkshire, Ted bought a large house there, Lumb Bank. But after a short time he returned to Court Green, and I spent Christmas 1963 there with Ted, the children Frieda and Nicholas, and Olwyn. There were also two guests, Tasha Hollis and Susan Alliston, who shared a flat in Great Ormond Street, one street away from Rugby Street, in London. Ted befriended Susan, who had been married to an American academic for a time and was courted by other men before her death from Hodgkin's disease in August 1969. After her death, Ted and Daniel Weissbort recovered a sheaf of poems from her flat in Rugby Street, where she had moved. Some poems were very good. A few of them were published in *Saint Botolph's Review*, no.2, 2006, and most or all were recovered and published by Richard Hollis in 2010.* Tasha and Susan went back to London after Christmas and I stayed on until mid-March.

While I was at Court Green we had a frequent visitor, Elizabeth Compton (now Sigmund), who had children about the ages of Frieda and Nicholas. She had been a helpful friend to Sylvia before her death during the eleven months they knew each other and often took care of Sylvia and Ted's children. She would drop by three times a day until Olwyn told her that once was enough. Elizabeth was married to David Compton, who had sold a mystery novel just before I arrived. It relieved their straitened circumstances and made it possible for him to put on spats for dinner, a story Olwyn and Ted loved to tell. David was a man of some dignity whom we saw less often than Elizabeth.

For a time, Elizabeth and David had moved into Court Green to show it to prospective buyers. No sale materialized. While they were in residence there Ted wrote four letters to David and Elizabeth, in an

*Susan Alliston: Poems and Journals, 1960-1969, with an Introduction by Ted Hughes. Nottingham: Five Leaves, 2010

excessively plain-spoken style, which Elizabeth sold to the British Library in 2002. David later gave an interview to Edward Butscher, Sylvia's first biographer, and subsequently wrote to him to protest at the use to which he had put the interview and to emphasize that he had explicitly warned him against Elizabeth's lively sense of the dramatic.*

Elizabeth knew what was going on behind every door in North Tawton, a small town whose old church was separated from Court Green by a solid stone wall. It was twenty miles from Elizabeth and David's house. She had friends everywhere and put me in mind of one of Chekhov's three sisters longing to get to Moscow but never getting there. When Sylvia came to Devon, a literary figure from London had suddenly appeared at a house not too far away. Elizabeth was the sort of friend anyone would want to have – she always agreed and never questioned you. Sylvia dedicated *The Bell Jar* to her and David.

At Court Green regular mail came through the kitchen doorway, but Ted would drive over to Okehampton where he had taken a post-box (I assume to collect letters from Assia). By this time, he had learned to take steps to ensure his personal privacy. Ted and I often went up to London, leaving Olwyn to look after the house and children. She became impatient with this arrangement and left a year and a half after I did to set up her literary agency in London.

Assia came down to Court Green with Shura some time after Olwyn left. Ted wrote optimistically that Assia had got things in order at Court Green and that Sylvia's children, Frieda and Nicholas, had greatly taken to Shura. I left Devon and, over a year later, Ted's mother came down. Edith Hughes suffered increasingly from asthma and arthritis in Yorkshire, and it was likely that she would benefit from a milder climate. Once the newsagents' shop was sold, his father joined them. There was an interlude for Ted of several months in Ireland (without his mother and father, who stayed at Court Green). The 'tribe' returned to Devon.

Tension mounted at Court Green, and Assia later told me that Willie Hughes would not speak to her or look at her when she put a

*
Butscher, Edward. *Sylvia Plath: The Woman and the Work.* New York: Dood, Mead, 1977; London: Peter Owen, 1979

plate of food in front of him. Edith Hughes, who was in bed downstairs or in the hospital at Exeter, could not accept Assia's presence any more easily than her husband.

Ted's parents' dislike of Assia was in their bones and she was aware of it. Ted dealt with the British class system as 'social rancour', and whenever Assia opened her mouth she put Ted's father in mind of it. I never understood how such otherwise good parents could make things difficult for Assia at a time when Ted most needed support, whereas they had been tolerant of Sylvia's peculiarities. But I think the essential reason was, in Ted's words, that her accent was his father's enemy. Assia was the mother of their grandchild and it could be that Ted's living with a thrice-married woman was unacceptable. In London, Assia made friends easily and was good company, but she did not succeed in making herself congenial to the Hughes parents. I never saw the four of them together and never worked it out. Sylvia had a knack, before and after she died, of making people aware of her side of things and Assia had no countervailing technique. Sylvia was acceptable, Assia unacceptable.

Soon Ted was writing that the place had become an 'inferno'. I never heard the parents' side of the story, but this was Ted's house, Olwyn was in London, Gerald in Australia, and Edith Hughes was often in hospital in Exeter and not well enough to go back to Yorkshire before the autumn of 1968. In the latter part of 1967, Ted wrote to me that he had taken 'Napoleonic' steps and sent Assia and Shura back to live in London. Assia and Shura died in March 1969 and, two months later, Ted's mother died in a hospital in Yorkshire. Ted's father returned to Devon.

In 1976 Ted's father went with Ted to Australia and stayed with Gerald in Melbourne while Ted went on alone to take part in the Adelaide Literary Festival. His father stayed in Australia for only four months, and when he came back, he lived in London with Olwyn for a time before returning to Devon. Ted was the responsible child again and he found a small house in the village for his father, who declined and became forgetful, and died in 1981.

Ted married Carol Orchard in August 1970. I met Carol when she was nineteen, tall and good looking. A wedding celebration in London brought together Ted's old Cambridge friends, and Dan Huws wrote to me that she sat through it 'like an angel'. Ted bought a farm near Court Green in 1972 and wrote that Carol and her father, a farmer who had come out of retirement, did all the work. (In fact, Ted liked to be out of doors and did a great deal of the work.) It was an interlude that lasted until February 1976, when Jack Orchard died of cancer. Carol grieved and Ted, who had become exceedingly fond of him, wrote extraordinary poems in Jack Orchard's memory. Jack Orchard was a natural man and *Moortown Diary* was dedicated to him. Some of the best poems in the volume are about his death and life and the volume as a whole has a starkness that sets it off from the collections of urban and literary poets. Ted wrote this book as the events on the farm happened, at once, and did not labour over them. This was unlike Sylvia's earlier poems but, in respect to immediacy, like her late poems.

After he came out of a black state he had never known before, brought on by the deaths of Assia and Shura, Ted became somewhat untethered. I have known Carol much longer but not as well as I had known Sylvia and Assia, but I knew that Ted would have fared badly without the anchor of the house, Court Green, and Carol.

Accusations

About a year after Sylvia died, Ted took me to meet Al Alvarez. When Sylvia died, Alvarez, the poetry critic of the *Observer*, had written a tribute to her, concluding with the line, 'The loss to literature is inestimable'. He was easy in company and had a fluent charm.

Alvarez liked Ted's first book, *The Hawk in the Rain*, and, even more, his second book, *Lupercal*, and gave them good reviews. He gave Sylvia's first book, *The Colossus*, a good but qualified review. The instinct for 'gentility' inhabited British postwar poetry and he was an early and articulate challenger of 'gentility'. A handful of rebels wrote in a full-throated style but Ted was the first to break through gentility to wide attention.

In his memoirs Alvarez writes that it was his custom to get to know authors, although, as the *Observer*'s poetry critic, he made a point of not getting to know poets he published.* But he got to know Ted and then Sylvia, although he saw them less than is supposed. I heard Ted's sister, Olwyn, also Sylvia's posthumous agent, speculate that he had seen Sylvia only six times in her life; the actual figure must have been about twelve, but these were at crucial junctures.

Sylvia sent Ted away from Court Green at the end of September 1962. He turned up to gather his things a few days later and Sylvia hired Susan O'Neill-Roe, a cheerful and patient twenty-two-year-old nurse who would not have to return to her hospital in London until mid-December. Everyone was fond of Susan and with the help of Elizabeth Compton she procured for Sylvia the freedom to go up to London from time to time. Sylvia, as noted by Richard Murphy in his appendix to *Bitter Fame*, had originally been planning to go to Ireland but had changed her mind.**

* Alvarez, A. *Where Did It All Go Right?* London: Richard Cohen, 1999

** Stevenson, Anne. *Bitter Fame: A Life of Sylvia Plath*. Boston: Houghton Mifflin; London: Penguin, 1989, appendix III

During the next weeks, Sylvia wrote many of her most famous poems. When she was in London, she brought some of them to Alvarez and read them to him. Sylvia intended them to be read aloud. She and Alvarez liked each other, but human emotions are complex and readers of the journals will know that Sylvia was aware of the tastes of editors and had been aware of them for years, from the time she began to keep a journal. It was desirable for a poet to appear in the pages of the *Observer*.

In 1971, eight years after Sylvia died, Alvarez published an essay about suicide, the first of two instalments, both of which were later incorporated into his book *The Savage God*.* The instalment and book started with Sylvia's suicide and the book's success propelled its author to wider recognition. He had been writing it for four years but had not shown any of it to Ted, although he had said he would. When Ted saw the first instalment in the *Observer*, he was astonished that someone he considered a friend would use private information to write a book. Frieda was eleven and Nicholas was nine and he had not told them how their mother had died; he collected them from school to tell them before they picked it up on the school playground. In an exchange of bitter letters quoted by Janet Malcolm, Alvarez wrote to Ted, 'As for the children, God knows that is an appallingly difficult thing. ... I did not know you had not yet told them about it, but there is no way in which they won't eventually find out'.** In his interview with Malcolm, he said, '... I suspect that what was driving him crazy was the realization that, however tactfully handled, this was public-domain stuff. The death had kind of put her into the public domain, do you see what I mean?'

Sylvia, especially by her suicide, had put herself in the public domain. Anne Sexton told her psychiatrist that Sylvia had beaten her to it. Alvarez had merely capitalized on her suicide more effectively than other journalists and Ted, at the age of forty, had not yet taken into account the fundamental priorities of London journalists. He was still enough of a Yorkshireman and little enough of a Londoner to ask the *Observer* to suppress the second instalment, without

*
Alvarez, A.
The Savage God,
London:
Weidenfeld and
Nicolson, 1971

**
Malcolm, Janet.
*The Silent
Woman: Sylvia
Plath and Ted
Hughes*. New
York: Knopf,
1993; London:
Picador, 1994
pp.123-30

reckoning that its suppression would increase sales of the book once it came out, which it did, the same year.

Over the twenty-two years that followed the appearance of *The Savage God*, Ted's personal reputation declined steadily, though by 1984 it had not reached a point that prevented his being named Poet Laureate. By 1994, when Janet Malcolm's book about Sylvia, *The Silent Woman*, developed from an article in the *New Yorker*, most people in the United States and some in the United Kingdom regarded Ted as a malefactor of women. Apart from *Bitter Fame*, the biography of Sylvia by Anne Stevenson, just about everything that appeared in print had suggested that he was. Malcolm, though, seemed to start afresh, interviewed and followed sources, read letters, and grasped most of a complicated story.

Long into his career, money continued to be Ted's enemy. One of several schemes in Cambridge days had been to establish a mink farm. He believed it would pay for itself in a short time. Later, he encouraged Gerald, and separately me, to raise cattle in Yorkshire. When Sylvia's literary remains began to become profitable, he found the estate was liable for an enormous tax, pursued for the government by an official named Mrs Skinner. 'Why does everything have to be so symbolical?' he wrote.

Janet Malcolm had developed sympathy for Ted by reading some of his letters, but she found her heart hardening towards him in reading others. In a letter to Aurelia explaining the futility of opposing the publication of *The Bell Jar* in the United States, she found that 'he had exchanged his right to privacy for a piece of real estate'.* Ted knew, of course, that it would be very unpleasant for Aurelia to have the book published in America but he wrote to her about buying 'an unbelievably beautiful place' on the north coast of Devon with the eventual proceeds. This was recognizably one of his optimistic schemes and he never bought the beautiful place. Malcolm read the letter at the Lilly Library with an indecipherable note by Aurelia on it. She needn't have hardened her heart. The note had been misread, and in a later edition, Malcolm made the correction.

* Malcolm, *op. cit.*, Note in British edition, dated 4 May 1994, pp. 209-213

Most of Ted's letters were not about practical affairs. What was unusual about them was the originality and acuity of the ideas they expressed, and, as if by accident, the generosity they conveyed. Nevertheless, a selection of them was not published until 2007. He liked to write letters; he could put his thoughts down without offering a polished object as he would with a poem for publication, and he could come back to his line of thinking later, or not come back to it, as he chose. He seems to have answered the many letters he received from schoolboys and schoolgirls, old Yorkshire friends, and known and unknown associates.

Ted's exchange of letters with Alvarez, however, fell into another category. Alvarez had sent Malcolm to the British Library, a surprising bit of unwariness, unless he did not appreciate that the letters made him look bad. Alvarez, in his reply to Ted's protest in relation to *The Savage God*, had said: 'It was written with great care and as a tribute to Sylvia ... among other reasons to lay some of the wild fantasies which are current about her death, fantasies which I imagine you must have heard more than I...' *

Why did Ted get himself into this situation? Once in it, why did he not realize that his trust had been given too easily? In 1971, he seemed to be trying to make Alvarez understand the offence. In the early 1990s, he wrote, 'Lucas, why did not someone tell me?' Ted had replied to Alvarez, 'You say I know perfectly well the memoir is not a piece of sensationalism. Easily said. I do not know that at all – and neither do you.' He went on to write, '... you say your article was written with care, but with what sort of care? I see care only of a very narrow technical sort – care to get the tone right and keep it right, and I can believe that was difficult, and depressing too...' At that time, Ted thought that it would have been depressing rather than recognizing it as an exercise in skill, a calculation that friendship with Ted would have to be given up to take advantage of a larger opportunity. And further on Ted writes, 'As for your article laying the wild fantasies, you know the opposite is much more likely. Before this, the fantasies were hot air, blowing each other away as fast as they were invented, all of

* Malcolm, *op. cit.*, carries an account of the exchange, pp.124-30

them perfectly weightless...' In the years that followed, Ted would recognize that the fantasies were empty but they were not weightless.

The Savage God opens with the prologue about Sylvia and closes with an epilogue about Alvarez's own suicide attempt. It is different from *The Bell Jar* in that it took four years rather than three months to write, and like it in that it was successful without answering any questions about the nature of suicide. Sylvia's attempt of 24 August 1953 was intended to be successful, he writes, whereas her completed suicide of 11 February 1963 was intended to be interrupted. This was Ted's theory immediately after Sylvia's suicide; it was communicated to Alvarez, but in time Ted regarded it as mistaken. It was a way of dealing with the survivor's grief and self-recrimination. However, Alvarez built the narrative he put into *The Savage God* on this theory, did not consult Ted, and later did not want to undermine what he had so successfully written. In this way, it is like the books of Sylvia's unquestioning admirers, for most of whom Alvarez was 'oracular'. He, in what he presented as a contrite passage, blames himself for 'letting her down unforgivably' but he is anxious to lead us to the conclusion that he was a critic who saw things others did not see. Ted later concluded that Sylvia's suicide was not preventable and Assia's was.

Alvarez did not deal in blame except in the relatively rare cases where the narrative of *The Savage God*, his interview with Janet Malcolm, and his memoir of 1999 were challenged. Then he did: Ted became 'barmy'; Assia, a fellow Jew but one who had escaped Hitler and was dead by the time Alvarez was writing, became 'rapacious'; and Anne Stevenson, who wrote *Bitter Fame* and in that process came to disagree with Ted's sister and agent Olwyn, wrote with a 'huge element of unconscious envy'. It was a minor poet's envy of a major poet, Alvarez told Malcolm. (Several decades later, Stevenson had won a number of prizes for her poetry although she was never as highly regarded as Sylvia.) His exchange of letters with Olwyn was published in the *New York Review of Books*; his letters were level-headed and convincing, hers full of exasperation.* Olwyn, he wrote, was 'unstoppable'. He told Malcolm that he had initiated a

*
New York Review of Books, 26 October 1989, 18 January 1990

'reappraisal' – that would be of *Bitter Fame*. Stevenson's book, some of which had been written or suggested by Olwyn, is now often discounted. Malcolm implies over-charitably that cordial relations between Ted and Alvarez were ultimately regained. I doubt that.

Alvarez wrote factually about the relationship between Ted and Sylvia until he ran up against something that would complicate the narrative of *The Savage God* and his autobiography, at which point he wrote artfully. In his interview with Malcolm, Alvarez said, 'Ted kind of went through swaths of women, like a guy harvesting corn. Sylvia must have known that.' In fact, Sylvia did not know that. If Sylvia had known that, she would presumably have reacted the same way she did six years after the wedding when Ted slept with Assia. It was, in part, a question of hanging on to Ted. Earlier, as her journals show, she was willing to have Sassoon sleep with a Swiss girl if he would also come back to her.* With Ted, after six years of marriage, it was a question of holding on to him, but she presented it as a question of adultery.

Alvarez's interview with Malcolm came almost three decades after Sylvia died. Apparently it was important to maintain the thesis of *The Savage God*. Just as Alvarez did not know Sylvia profoundly, Ted did not know Alvarez very well or very critically in 1971, but that did not prevent Alvarez from telling Malcolm,

> As I remember, I was terribly hurt by Ted's letters, because, one, I had assumed he was a good friend and, two, he knew as well as I that I had bent over backward, almost – but not quite – to the level of falsifying the evidence, to keep the business of their marriage breakup out of my account.**

Alvarez did not falsify the evidence because he did not know Sylvia well enough to have the evidence.

In *The Savage God*, Sylvia was bright and transatlantic and a genius recognized by few. She was also a troubled woman. Understandably, as Alvarez confided in Janet Malcolm's interview, he did not want the responsibility of taking on a troubled woman. He goes on to confess that she was not his physical type. An alternative explanation would be that he sidestepped an entanglement and, after

* Plath, *Johnny Panic and the Bible of Dreams*, 'Cambridge Notes', p.203

** Malcolm, *op. cit.*, p.130

seeing her a few times in October and November, avoided all further meetings – except on Christmas Eve, when he stopped by on the way to a party at V. S. Pritchett's, left in spite of her tears, and did not return her telephone call afterwards. Next thing he heard was that she had died, whereupon he wrote an appreciation of her in the *Observer*, accompanied Ted to the coroner's on 15 February, did not go up to Yorkshire for the funeral and, a few years later, used her case to begin his book on suicide. He did not know her well enough to understand her mentality or her reasons for committing suicide. *Birthday Letters*, which regularly mythologizes Sylvia, gets it right in the conclusion to 'The 59th Bear'. If she could not assign death to a figure in a poem, as is the case in this poem, she assigned it to herself. It was an essential part of her rationalization, and never questioned that stage of her ego and therefore never got beyond it.

As time passed, Alvarez had to undergird what he had said in the Malcolm interview and written in his autobiography, with a sense of Ted. Ted could not be portrayed as ordinary. Alvarez isolated two characteristics that contained some measure of truth: the first that he was superstitious and the second that he was a womanizer. In the memoir, Alvarez wrote, '...he seemed to have easy, immediate access to his source of inspiration'. something that set him apart 'from most young poets of his generation, even from Plath when they first met...' He continued,

> *The weird mishmash of astrology, black magic, Jung, Celtic myth and pagan superstition that got him to where he wanted to be worked fine for him ... but for Sylvia it was a foreign country in every sense ... Belief in dark gods and shamans and the baleful influence of the stars didn't come naturally to her...**

Ted loved astrology but Sylvia and I, though willing, could never get ourselves deeply involved in it. We were Americans and, especially in our generation, the assumption we had absorbed was that everything should be demonstrable and, if it weren't, should be discarded. For Ted, astrology was a dramatic language for describing human nature,

* Alvarez, *Where Did It All Go Right? op. cit.*, p.203

a symbolic language, and a programme for action or inaction. He would have put that in poetic language unless forced to write for cash in a review, as he was in 'Superstitions', a review of Louis MacNeice's *Astrology*.* In 'St Botolph's' (*Birthday Letters*), Chaucer himself would have stayed at home the day Ted met Sylvia, warned by the stars. In another formulation in the same poem, Chaucer sadly says that the solar system had married them whether they knew it or not. Ted's argument was rational but his taste was to use astrological symbols to describe variations in human behaviour.

Another explanation could be that their two temperaments married them – congenially for Ted and one that Sylvia accepted willingly enough. It gave shape, as she thought of it, to their joint destiny. As it turned out, it was not a propitious shape but it was one that produced poetry that appealed to many readers.

In the review of MacNeice's *Astrology*, Ted wrote that there are too many variables for astrology to set itself up as a science rather than an intuitive art. If it should be an esoteric science like advanced mathematics, as expert astrologers claim, it still did not make any difference to the generality as long as it worked. Science long ago had the good sense to conceal its failures. His thinking was clear enough (though guided by a love of astrological discourse) but he never went into his ideas prosaically enough to make them difficult to distort. Even his sympathetic biographer Elaine Feinstein labels him superstitious on one page, though not elsewhere. If there was a book to be published or a trip to be taken, he would usually choose a date identified by the stars. This method seems superstitious until the alternatives are considered: do not think about it and make no choice, or let the time be at the publisher's convenience, or let train schedules decide, or let market forces determine what will work out best.

Ted loved to give some metaphorical system to his instincts. In larger matters, he thought that truth could be formulated in the language of poetry and inadequately in prose, which was not bullion but false coin. What he thought of as bullion can be identified in his letters or in occasional prose, such as collected in *Winter Pollen*. He

* MacNeice, Louis. *Astrology*. London: Aldus; New York: Doubleday, 1964, reviewed by Ted Hughes in the *Listener*, 2 October 1964; reprinted in Ted Hughes. *Winter Pollen*, London: Faber, 1994, p.51ff.
*

was vulnerable in being seen as superstitious, and as a womanizer, by critics who had a case to make, by ideological opponents, and by jealous writers. In fact, his taste for the symbological structure of astrology usually submerged uncertainties and led him to speak metaphorically. His views are not literal. Or literalistic.

Reputations

From the 1970s until the end of Ted's life I was living in New York, San Francisco, and India and was not often in London. But from time to time I saw Daniel Weissbort, who had founded *Modern Poetry in Translation* with Ted and was then at the University of Iowa, and I corresponded with Ted and with Dan Huws. Ted had written to me that he had had a period of old-time 'folly', our word for irresponsible sleeping around. Sexual and professional jealousy were both apt to emerge in what was written about Ted.

I was told that London had divided into two camps, some in favour of Sylvia and some in favour of Ted, the camp favouring Ted being initially larger. Ted thought that it was intrusive to speculate about what went on between a husband and wife, yet the intrusions had only begun. After Assia and Shura died, public opinion shifted and became much less favourable to Ted. The downward line of his reputation, from Alvarez in 1971 to Janet Malcolm in 1993, progressed through a series of biographies of Sylvia.

It is hard to get trustworthy and historical information from anything that has been written about Sylvia or – unless the reader is unusually alert – anything she wrote. One of the best writers who tried to take the subject on asked me for an interview and I wrote to Ted. He said I should be wary of her and gave me the story of a reading he gave with Peter Redgrove in London. After the reading, they were invited for a drink at a house nearby and arrived to find a tempting table laid. Ted and Redgrove were sitting on the same sofa and talking uninhibitedly. 'What is that whirring?' Redgrove suddenly asked. They stood up and pulled the sofa back. Underneath, a tape recorder was recording their conversation. Thus forewarned, I asked the enquiring writer to meet me across the street in a restaurant. I declined to give her any information and she declined to let me pay for her lunch. She also wept. In retrospect, I should have suggested she forgo the use of a tape recorder and proceed with the biography. But she abandoned the project and came to the conclusion that this subject sent writers to the crazy house. I wondered if it was not so much a jinx as overcoming the subject's difficulties.

Five biographies of Sylvia were published in Ted's lifetime. The first, published in 1976, was by Edward Butscher, who found cooperative informants in the United States but few people willing to speak when he got to Great Britain.* I read the book (which had Assia as 'Olga'), and I bought the subsequent collection of essays on Sylvia which he edited, published the following year.** Ted believed that the original publisher, Seabury Press, had undertaken to publish Butscher's book of poems with the understanding that he would write a biography of Sylvia.

In his second book, Butscher included an essay by Joyce Carol Oates.*** Oates had not entirely worked out her ideas about Sylvia by 1974 yet had a better understanding of her mentality than most authors who came later. 'But', Oates wrote, 'she did not "like" other people because she did not essentially believe that they existed; she knew intellectually that they existed, of course, since they had the power to injure her, but she did not believe they existed in the way she did, as pulsating, breathing, suffering individuals.'

Butscher approached the Newnham lecturer, Dorothea Krook, for an essay since Sylvia greatly admired Krook, but the memoir reveals that Krook was reluctant because she did not know Sylvia well enough. At Cambridge, I shared Sylvia's admiration of Dr Krook and went to all her lectures. 'I only knew her', Krook wrote, 'really, as a beautiful, sensitive mind, ardently enjoying the exhilarations of the life of the intellect, living intensely, joyously, in the calm sunshine of the mind, as Hume calls it.' That does not sound like a girl who would bite a man she had just met at a party. It conveys the way in which one part of her – the part Krook saw – presented itself. Another part was

*
Butscher, Edward. *Sylvia Plath: Method and Madness*. New York: Seabury Press, 1976

**
Butscher, Edward. *Sylvia Plath: The Woman and the Work*. New York: Dood, Mead, 1977; London: Peter Owen, 1979

***
Reprinted from Oates, Joyce Carol. *New Heaven, New Earth: The Visionary Experience in Literature*. New York: Vanguard, 1974

loud, aggressive and exaggeratedly American, and this is what most fellow students at Cambridge saw.

Butscher himself commissioned five of the seventeen articles in his collection of essays. The author of one, Jane Baltzell (now Kopp), was in Sylvia's college, Newnham, and in her hall of residence, Whitstead, at Cambridge. Academically, she was thought to be even more gifted than Sylvia. She was an American blonde of German descent who resembled Sylvia and was about the same height, but whose demeanour was modest. One would expect her article to be carefully written and most of it is. Sylvia emerges essentially as I knew her; Jane emerges as putting up with difficult behaviour in order to perpetuate a friendship. But Sylvia came to see Jane as a 'doppelgänger', therefore a competitor.

When Sylvia is no longer the central figure, Jane's essay becomes less reliable. Ted and Jane knew each other only glancingly but he had met her before the incident of the early hours of 10 March, when we threw gravel up at a Whitstead window. I never heard him use four-letter words, or use the word 'prostitute', but he did use it on that night. He had seen Sylvia only once, on the night she had bitten his cheek. 'Compared to Jane, she's a prostitute', he said. But he did not feel that way long; he was soon 'so locked on you, so brilliantly / That everything that was not you was blind-spot' ('Fidelity', *Birthday Letters*). Jane wrote that Sylvia herself (as many women may) occasionally liked to think of herself as a 'whore' and in her journal entry for that Sunday, 11 March 1956, she sees herself as the Blanche DuBois of Tennessee Williams's *A Streetcar Named Desire*.

Ted and Olwyn did not like Butscher's book and they would like what came after it less. Linda Wagner (later Wagner-Martin), a feminist who had produced a biography in 1987, had preconceptions and a commonplace writing style.* Ronald Hayman, who was at Cambridge and met Ted there once, wrote a biography of Sylvia in 1991 that was factually inaccurate and impelled by hostility to Ted.** The same year *Rough Magic* came out, written by Paul Alexander, an American described by Olwyn in 1988 as 'a rather dreamy young

* Martin-Wagner, Linda. *Sylvia Plath: A Life*. London: Chatto & Windus, 1988

** Hayman, Ronald. *The Death and Life of Sylvia Plath*. London: Heinemann; New York: Birch Lane Press, 1991

man', blond with an earring.* Olwyn initially thought he might or might not be able to write a good biography but before long lowered her opinion. Ted told me that he had received $150,000 from Viking to write the book. It came out and implied, without saying so plainly, that Ted had hypnotized Sylvia into killing herself. It used 'confidential sources' without giving names.

The author of Sylvia's third biography, *Bitter Fame*, was Anne Stevenson, who back in Cambridge days had been married to Robin Hitchcock, my landlady's son. Much later, in the eighties, Anne was commissioned by Penguin to write a short life of Sylvia for the 'Lives of Modern Women' series. Olwyn got Anne much better terms for a full-scale biography with unrestricted access to Sylvia's papers. Anne sent a letter to Ted and received his agreement, but not an interview with him. Anne's book appeared in 1989. Collaborative work by the author, and Olwyn as agent, began cordially and ended in discord. It was the only one that at the time put Ted in a favourable light and was mediated by Sylvia's one-time lover, Peter Davison, the son of an English poet, who had grown up in the United States, gone to Harvard then Cambridge, emerged from New York into Boston, and edited the book for Houghton Mifflin. Davison had had an affair with Sylvia in the summer of 1955 that was not agreeable; it left him with the feeling of being 'used' and 'despised' (Sylvia had won a Fulbright grant and wanted information about Cambridge). Decades later, he had developed a more tolerant perspective.

The Haunting of Sylvia Plath, published in 1991 by a British scholar, Jacqueline Rose, was well received.** It presented itself as an examination of what Sylvia and Ted had written, as opposed to their personalities. I thought it would be forgotten after the momentary academic fashion passed but many (including Malcolm) thought it was significant.

In 1993 *The Silent Woman* by Janet Malcolm caused a revaluation; Ted's volume, *Birthday Letters*, 1998, made it stick. Andrew Motion, Ted's successor as Poet Laureate, wrote that Ted's book of poems had made him re-think Ted's reputation and he spoke for

---

* Alexander, Paul. *Rough Magic: A Biography of Sylvia Plath*. New York: Viking, 1991

** Rose, Jacqueline. *The Haunting of Sylvia Plath*. London: Little, Brown, 1992; Cambridge MA: Harvard University Press, 1993

others who had evaluated Ted and Sylvia and Assia's reputations. In a year or two, though, the grumbling began again, resurrecting the arguments heard after Assia's death. Reviewing *Bitter Fame*, Alvarez had written that '...the feminist vision of Plath as "a great woman artist who was abused, put upon, and betrayed by men" [was] in 'every respect...the crudest sentimentality",'.* The same critic who was seen as 'oracular' by women's liberationists, and had sent Malcolm down to see Elizabeth Compton in Cornwall, seemed to be forgiven for this observation or had it overlooked.

In 2003, several years before her death, Diane Middlebrook, a distinguished Stanford scholar, published a book about Sylvia and Ted called *Her Husband*.** Middlebrook had earlier written a biography of Anne Sexton. Although it used tapes of Sexton's sessions with a psychoanalyst who also wrote an introduction to the book, it had been well received.*** Middlebrook was interested in Sylvia and was drawn to the large number of Ted's papers at Emory University. She seemed to me to be affected by reading this archive at Emory and to become more sympathetic to Ted.

During her last four days, Sylvia stayed with Jillian Becker and her then husband, Gerry, both South African teachers and writers living in London. Forty years later, Jillian wrote a memoir called *Giving Up*.**** She was severely shaken by those four days, so shaken that (by her account) she changed permanently. Although she was a poet herself, she was alienated from poets and poetry. Jillian and Gerry went up to Heptonstall for the funeral; besides them, only Sylvia's brother and his wife and Ted and his family and one habitual churchgoer were there. Ted emerged from the memoir as a monster.

If Ted's patience had been taxed by the appearance of Alvarez's *The Savage God*, it was stretched much further in the next quarter century and he allowed himself to be called out into the bullring on one particularly trying occasion. The name 'Hughes' had been chiselled off Sylvia's tombstone in Heptonstall on three or four occasions and a letter saying that Sylvia was lying in an unmarked grave had been published in the newspapers. It was signed by Hayman,

* *New York Review of Books*, 28 September 1989

** Middlebrook, Diane Wood. *Her Husband: Hughes and Plath – A Marriage* New York: Viking, 2003; London:Little, Brown, 2004

*** Middlebrook, Diane Wood. *Anne Sexton: A Biography.* Boston MA: Houghton Mifflin, 1991

**** Becker, Jillian. *Giving Up: The Last Days of Sylvia Plath.* London: Ferrington, 2002; New York: St. Martin's Press, 2003

Alvarez and several others. Joseph Brodsky said, 'Not me,' disclaiming his signature, which seemed to have been added to the letter without his permission.

Apart from stating that Sylvia's monument had been defaced several times and was in the stonemason's shop, Ted could have suppressed his reply, but it is not surprising that he could not contain himself. Answering all the attacks would have been a full-time job and a futile one. If there had ever been a time for understanding Sylvia's personality, it had passed and the time for revaluation had not yet arrived – and may never arrive. In 1998, the year he died, Ted finally spoke publicly about the inheritors of Alvarez in 'The Dogs Are Eating Your Mother' (*Birthday Letters*). The perfect storm that Ted encountered – for which he also unknowingly created the conditions – did not exist solely because of feminism and could have existed without the women's movement. It was the quality and character of Sylvia's late poetry that generated it. Although it arrived in public attention at a good time, its underlying appeal was as a representation of readers' feelings. It was a justification of feelings that had been only half-realized until she expressed them, and their appeal was not confined to females.

The feminist movement produced change over two or three decades until militancy was no longer necessary. In literature, Sylvia was taken as an emblematic figure and although she was not really a feminist and the feminist movement did not get a good start until after she died, that did not seem to matter. Contradictions could be ignored because the movement was strong. After Sylvia committed suicide, Germaine Greer said, 'Ted Hughes existed to be punished – we had lost a heroine and we needed to blame someone...'* The package included an anti-heroine, Assia.

*
Quoted in
Brooke Allen,
'Ted Hughes:
In Sylvia's
Shadow',
*New York Times
Book Review*,
3 February
2002

But that was not the underlying fact and therefore could not last forever. What was lasting was the strength of Sylvia's poetry and its effectiveness in expressing anyone's wish – that is the wish of the ego – to state things favourable to the self. Everything was stated the way the ego wanted it stated and put so forcefully and unquestioningly

[87]

that it was believable. Sylvia's voice stated the self's case and readers subscribed to this because it expressed a side of themselves no one could express so well, and it inundated the other, more outer-directed sides of themselves. This was where the Ariel voice arrived, and it surprised Ted, who thought poetry was healing and a sure expression of the truth. As *Birthday Letters* developed, the truth had to be mythologized to be acceptable to Ted. No one else had as large or complete a vision.

Sylvia's universe was not social but inward-looking, with a single heroine. It was Sylvia's predicament in life – and a predicament that did not engage her curiosity and therefore did not explicitly enter her consciousness. Her mother, as *Letters Home* shows, reinforced Sylvia's concentration on herself. Richard Sassoon, the lover immediately before Ted, slept with her off and on for two years but disappeared in March 1956. Next there was Ted, who married her and developed a relationship that went beyond her self-involvement without making her confront it; he stirred her in an unprecedented way and stimulated her achievement. She planned to make their relationship the subject of a novel, but the poem 'Edge' concluded her creative – as well as her actual – life.

The year Ted died and a third of a century after Sylvia died, he expressed his thoughts in *Birthday Letters* and his thinking had considerably evolved and darkened over that time. But the contradictions between a mother who was 'the dearest of mothers' with the 'eely tentacle' and the father of 'Among the Bumblebees' with 'A man in black with a Meinkampf look' were never brought together or reconciled. In fact they were perpetuated by her psychiatrist, Dr Beuscher. In an utterly different way, Ted's mythologizing effectively reinforced Dr Beuscher's rationalization.

Ted wrote to me that he had dreamed disturbing dreams of Sylvia. For more than two decades, he continued to compose poems but he was undecided about publishing them. In 1993, he said that the ultimate release would be to make these poems public but it would bring down a new rain of imbecilities on his head. Most of the poems in

Birthday Letters had never been seen before. The poems were composed over a long period of time and they were not identical in tone, the later ones being more fatalistic – and more mythologized – than the earlier. He gave me a copy of *Birthday Letters* on 29 January 1998, the day it was published. Nine months later, he died.

    I liked *Birthday Letters* as well as but not better than one or two of his other volumes and wrote him a letter of appreciation, but I criticized one poem, 'Dreamers', which I said should be shorter or rewritten. Of course it could not be shorter or rewritten. Assia had described her premonitory dream; 'Dreamers' in *Birthday Letters* says that Ted could interpret it but the others could not. My objection was that it put Assia in a bad light. 'Dreamers' was Sylvia's view of Assia.

Otto and Aurelia

Sylvia had contradictory feelings about her father and mother. Otto Plath, Sylvia's father, was twenty-one years older than her mother, who had been his student. He was born in Grabow, a Prussian town in the Polish Corridor and, aged sixteen, emigrated to the United States. After a year with an uncle in New York, he went out to Wisconsin where his grandparents lived and embarked on the study of divinity. But he read Darwin, and when he decided against becoming a Lutheran minister, his name was struck from the family bible. He wound up with a PhD in entomology from Harvard and a teaching post at Boston University and he published an authoritative book called *Bumblebees and Their Ways*. Otto knew five languages, taught biology and German, insisted on doing all the shopping, and spread his books over one end of the dining-room table where Sylvia's mother, Aurelia, was told they were not to be disturbed.

What I think was Sylvia's best story, 'Among the Bumblebees', written when she was about twenty, describes a strong man whom his daughter loves and who loves his daughter. 'Among the Bumblebees' says, 'For Alice Denway's father had been a giant of a man.' Sylvia had written the story when she was twenty. 'Alice worshipped her father because he was so powerful, and everybody did what he commanded because he knew best and never gave mistaken judgment.'

Otto Plath had not seen his first wife for fifteen years when he was divorced from her and married Aurelia Schober, who was to become Sylvia's mother. Otto had been in America several decades when his health began to decline. He thought he had cancer and refused to give in to it or acknowledge it publicly. The disease turned out to be diabetes and it killed him in 1940. He was fifty-three.

When Otto Plath died their mother had two children and no resources; Warren was two and a half years younger than Sylvia, who had just turned eight. In 'Among the Bumblebees' he was her baby brother, but Warren grew to be a tall and able-bodied young man who went to Exeter and Harvard on scholarship and became a scientist. In Sylvia's story Warren is indulged by the mother, whereas Alice Denway is her father's favourite.

Sylvia's maternal grandparents moved in with Aurelia and her children after Otto's death. Aurelia resumed teaching and saw the children through school. She had no sense of humour, absorbed the moralism of New England, combined it with her Teutonic inheritance, and brought the children along to the point where they gained entrance into Smith and Harvard. Sylvia's expenses at McLean and her scholarship at Smith were funded by Olive Higgins Prouty, who was temperamentally the opposite of Sylvia's mother. Prouty had suffered from a nervous breakdown and been institutionalized when she was young. Sylvia's experience was one that Prouty imagined she herself had undergone.

Not everything Ted says in his letters should be taken literally or used as a source by biographers. He had once described Aurelia Plath as 'an extraordinary woman'.* This was not something he would have written in 1963 when he found her letters encouraging Sylvia to get a divorce, or in the late 1980s and 1990s when he wrote to me wondering why he had coddled Sylvia and responded to Aurelia's overriding wish to be seen as a dedicated mother who had sacrificed her life for her children. She lived a joyless life and invested her expectations in her children. Although her letters eliciting Sylvia's have reportedly been burned, we can tell something about them from what Sylvia wrote.

Sylvia wrote in her journal that Dr Beuscher gave her 'permission' to hate her mother in December 1958; on 16 October 1962, Sylvia wrote 'Medusa', which ends, 'Off, off, eely tentacle! / There is nothing between us.' It was the same day she wrote a letter to her mother saying, 'I am a genius of a writer; I have it in me. I am writing the best

*
Hughes, *Letters*, Letter to Anne Sexton, 9 August 1967, p.275

poems of my life; they will make my name.' Sylvia both loved and hated her mother, but her letters were written not actually for Aurelia but as rationalizations of her own behaviour. They were public and made her case publicly to her mother as stand-in for the world. Another case, parallel but not identical, was set forth in the journals and dealt with questions she was trying to resolve, matters such as her ambition and her assessment of individual men. Ted said she could 'not be helped' that way – that way being reacting to her rationalizations. Although she could not be helped that way, it was the stuff of poems that made her famous.

By the end of her life, Sylvia was able to bring an entire poem into unity or meaning. She had developed a capacity to bring all the allusions and inferences into a unified whole, such as the 'eely tentacle' she was speaking of in 'Medusa' or the 'Panzer-man' in 'Daddy'. Written on 12 October 1962, a decade after 'Among the Bumblebees', the poem ends, 'Daddy, daddy, you bastard, I'm through.' In an interview with the BBC, she explained that the speaker in 'Daddy' was schizophrenic, but in fact what enabled the poem to be written was not schizophrenia but resentment against other human beings (her father, whom she lost just before she was eight, and, by extension, her husband). Similarly, the loss of her mother in 'Medusa' was the definitive loss of a correspondent she had once had. She offered her mother accomplishments in the hope of gaining a mother's love, but the letters are false, and so she welcomed Dr Beuscher's permission to hate her mother. At the same time she loved her mother, and Sylvia could never reconcile the two emotions or bring them together, either with her mother or anyone else.

The Ariel voice

Sylvia's journal records that she wrote 'Pursuit' on 27 February 1956. This was less than two days after she met Ted at the *Saint Botolph's Review* party and she had not seen him a second time. It was one of the best poems she had written up to that time and it was about sex: a panther – in fact a man – climbing the stairs to possess a woman violently. It was also immature. Sylvia was twenty-three; we all took a long time to mature in our generation and twenty-three was young. Sylvia's surviving journals, published in 2000, give the background of this period.* The journals were not a factual diary and, if read literally, will be confusing, but they can be disentangled, although that will require discrimination from future scholars. On a single page you may find exercises in fiction, historical fact, speculations about people, and drafts of unsent letters all jumbled together. The essential historical facts are: 25 February 1956, Saint Botolph's party; 27 February, composed 'Pursuit'; 10 and 11 March, Ted and I threw gravel at what we mistakenly thought was her window in her hall of residence; 23 and 24 March, Sylvia and Ted slept together in London; 24 March through 13 April, Sylvia was on the Continent, looking for but not finding Richard Sassoon, and proceeded to Rome with Gordon Lameyer; 13 to 17 April, Sylvia was at Ted's flat in London; 17 April, Sylvia returned to Cambridge; about 25 April or soon after, Ted came up to Cambridge and stayed at Tenison Road; 10 May or soon after, Sylvia asked Ted to marry her and he agreed but did not tell anyone; 16 June, Sylvia and Ted were married in London.

On 21 April, Sylvia wrote 'Ode for Ted'. It described him as familiar with nature but it was less successful as poetry than 'Pursuit', which was entirely believable. Ted told me a week or two later that she

*Plath, *Journals*, pp.214–46 and appendices 7, 8 and 9

was writing 'embarrassing' poems about him, yet that did not alter his feelings for her, which grew visibly that May. He believed in her talent; friends noticed the artificiality but he seemed to treat it, as far as I could judge, as something her innermost self would overcome. The force of his personality may have broken through the artificiality and washed it aside to expose an essential self, but more than one essential self existed side by side and the self of Sylvia's that wrote the poems in the Ariel voice was not the one Ted was expecting. The physical connection may have overwhelmed other things (a matter for speculation), but I do not think sex was more important than their congeniality. Once Ted spoke to me of physical love as a means of resolving lovers' quarrels, so both elements must have been in play.

In October 1959, Ted thought she was breaking through to her essential voice, the one that developed into the Ariel voice. In 1962, she broke through in a marked way. That autumn, she was making poems out of their 'bad moments together' – and these were the best poems she had ever written. It was a strong voice and it led to her death and overshadowed the rest of Ted's life. This register of the Ariel voice was propelled by jealousy and possessiveness and Sylvia affected his feelings more than any other woman in his lifetime. In Sylvia's poems the talent and discipline were there from the start but usually not as a completed poem. The early and middle academic images weren't like her everyday self, but most of her poems were snared in that language and imagery. A few succeeded, ironically including the one I found open on the top of the wardrobe in Assia's flat, 'Metaphors', the nine lines of which included 'I've eaten a bag of green apples' and 'Boarded the train there's no getting off'. She probably was still only capable of thinking of other persons as 'counterparts' to her own self, but when she was with Ted there must have been something in their intimate relations that carried her beyond it. In Ted's absence, she could proceed to the bitterness, then the nullity, of both registers of the Ariel voice. With Ted, she was helped by his suggestions and by living very closely with him. Motherhood was not the fundamental theme; she killed herself when

Frieda was less than three and Nicholas was thirteen months old. The poems into which the children enter were essentially 'rhetorical' (in Joyce Carol Oates's word), whereas 'Daddy' and 'Medusa' were pure and totally successful vessels of resentment and hate for her father, her husband and her mother. They were the voice of a defined personality in a play which was only about her. Sylvia was the mother of the 'baby in the barn' who committed suicide when the baby was thirteen months old ('Nick and the Candlestick', *Ariel*). The expressions of hate and resentment and of affection or love in letters addressed to her 'Dearest of Mothers', in the father of 'Among the Butterflies', and in Ted as the panther of 'Pursuit' were never brought into a unified set of feelings. Dr Beuscher very likely did not understand this adequately. Sylvia's suicide was not brought on by sexual jealousy but by rationalized and frustrated possessiveness.

How was it that Ted was deaf to all this? Cohen was not deaf to it but he had been dismissed years before in favour of Beuscher. Sylvia had become involved, though not meaningfully, with other men, as her journals from the age of seventeen make clear. Sassoon disappeared; the previous March (1956), she had been willing to return to him if she could have found him, in spite of the Swiss girl she thought he was living with. Ted married her in June 1956. My understanding is that she was willing to sleep with at least two men between September and the end of November 1962, and did sleep with one of them. Ted described himself as a 'public adulterer' to me, but it was not his adultery that caused Sylvia to write to her mother, her aunt and Mrs Prouty that she was thinking of divorce. It was her possessiveness.

Before Ted

'I could not help being amazed that artistry of such stature could have emerged from so deficient a personality,' Peter Davison wrote in his memoir *Half Remembered*.* 'But art, one comes to learn, can gain as much from pressure as from depth.' Davison, as poetry editor of the *Atlantic Monthly*, received new poems from the girl with whom he had conducted an affair seven years before. The artistry he discovered was in the creation of the late poems. At the end of the 1980s, he edited *Bitter Fame* for Houghton Mifflin and it was then I had some correspondence with him.

Sylvia was about to go to Cambridge and Davison had been a student there. 'Her quest for knowledge was voracious,' he wrote, 'I felt as though I were being cross-examined, drained, eaten; yet when she told me about her life, her previous love affairs, her successes at Smith, it was as though she were describing a stranger to herself, a highly trained circus horse.' She described the suicide attempt of August 1953: 'What I heard was a simpler, less poised, and more touching story' – more touching than the account in *The Bell Jar*. It was the only time he felt he was able to connect with Sylvia as a human being. But she broke the affair off and it is noticeable that Davison does not tell his readers, given the way he felt, why he allowed it to go on as long as it did. It may be that he found the same fascination in her that Jane Baltzell did – or lovers like Ted's predecessors and Ted himself did.

There must have been something about Sylvia – obsession mixed, improbably, with detachment – that attracted Richard Sassoon. He fled more than once, the final time after their Christmas and New Year's trip together to the south of France on his motorcycle. Richard

* Davison, Peter. *Half Remembered: A Personal History.* New York: Harper & Row, 1973; London: Heinemann, 1974

[96]

had met Sylvia in the spring of 1954 and conducted an affair with her, sporadically, until the beginning of 1956. This was a period during which she was also having affairs with Davison and Gordon Lameyer. Richard weighed no more than Sylvia but, in spite of the fact that height and weight were important to her, he was the only man with whom she was deeply engaged until she met Ted. Once her involvement with Ted began, she apparently thought of him no more.

Elsewhere in his memoir, Davison said, 'Poetry is a gift, not a role.' Sylvia was gifted and the 'role' of poet was, at the most, secondary to the 'pressure' registered in her journals, pressure for publication and money. There was pressure to write the poems and inordinate pressure to have them published. In 1955, when Davison and Sylvia had their affair, she showed him poems that 'were not yet poems'. The technical gift was there but not yet the authenticity of impulse.

Gordon Lameyer, after they had broken up, saw her as 'narcissistic' and 'schizophrenic' and believed that the loss of her father when she was a child prevented her from loving anyone fully. It may be that Sylvia was a different person before her suicide attempt of 24 August 1953, but I doubt it. No change is plain from her journals: the pressure is constant. Whether she was genetically abnormal or her abnormality developed as she was growing up (perhaps as a result of the influence of her unfortunate mother) is unknowable. I suspect that it was the latter. Her father's death when she was just eight, sad as that is, cannot be the central cause since people have lost one or both parents in wars or plagues or by bad luck since the beginning of time and do not therefore see themselves as unconnected to others.

Sylvia's boyfriends' view of events could be understood from what they wrote. Among those she slept with, Peter Davison remembered 'her chilly touch, the fingers of the succubus' although he does not explain why his affair with her went on until she stopped it. Gordon Lameyer wound up writing that she was 'schizophrenic' and Richard Sassoon disappeared without leaving a forwarding address.

The Fifty-Ninth Bear

Sylvia, who would give birth to Frieda Rebecca on 1 April 1960, did not join the farewell to me, bound for New Orleans, on 18 March, but Ted, Dan and Helga Huws, and other members of the Saint Botolph's group, saw me to the ship's gangway.

I was in the United States for two years and while I was there I came across a short story by Sylvia, 'The Fifty-Ninth Bear', in the *London Magazine*.* It was inspired by her trip with Ted across the continent in the summer of 1959 and I had heard of the adventure before, but not as Sylvia presented it. Her story gave me pause. In Yellowstone Park, Sadie and Norton, recognizable versions of Sylvia and Ted, agree to play a game: counting bears for a ten-dollar wager. She thinks they will see fifty-nine, he seventy-one. In their last night in the park, the two of them are in a sleeping bag in their tent and a bear approaches, snuffles at the tent, and breaks the rear window of the car to get at the fish and oranges there. Norton goes out with his light to chase the bear away and shines the light in its eyes. But the fifty-ninth bear does not move away; it comes close enough to smash Norton with its huge arm. Norton tastes blood as he dies.

It is not unprecedented for the subconscious to produce a dream or daydream of a husband or father or brother, or a wife, mother or sister (if the dreamer is a man) dying. If it comes, you recognize it and try to deal with it and dispel it, and if it won't go away you ordinarily disguise the characters before making a story of it. I never discussed 'The Fifty-Ninth Bear' with Ted but I mentioned my reaction to it the next time I saw Olwyn and it seemed to have the same disturbing effect on her as on me. When I read *Birthday Letters* more than a third of a century later, I found a poem called 'The 59th Bear'. He had

*Reprinted in *Johnny Panic and the Bible of Dreams*, 1977

not realized, the poem said, how death was moving in her head and had to find a place to alight temporarily before it resumed its flight and landed somewhere else and then somewhere else.

Why did not Ted confront her idea and deal with it right away? Why did he keep it down so long? Some part of the answer – not the whole it – was in the disposition of a last-born child married to a first-born. Another part was his realization that I had reservations about Sylvia. Yet another was that we did not talk about it, that I had greater reservations about her than he did, that we might not have agreed entirely, and that he did not subscribe to my reservations or think I fully understood her. In any case, Ted did not talk about her analytically, possibly because he thought I did not fully understand her or else was not sympathetic to her.

'We are amazingly compatible,' Sylvia wrote in her journal.* Although I had always found them amazingly different, Ted and Sylvia, for most of their marriage, thought of themselves as complements to each other and they often said as much. Sylvia wrote incisively in her journals about people as members of some species under review, not in the same basket as the one she lived in.

We do not invariably see compatibility in the journals, though. 'I enjoy it when Ted is off for a bit,' she wrote. 'I must be myself – make myself & not let myself be made by him.' Ted gave orders: read ballads for an hour, Shakespeare for an hour, history for an hour, think for an hour and read nothing in bits but straight through. Ted would ask her, 'What are you going to do now?' and 'What are you thinking now?' She believed that objective witnesses like Leonard Baskin agreed with her about Ted's fanaticism and lack of balance and moderation. Ted tended to suck her into a 'disastrous whirlpool'.**

It was as though there were no barriers between them and one of them kept abrading the other. Being married to him was stimulating but it exhausted her reserves, which for years had been radically taxed by her own demands. Her impulse to keep others at arms' length from Ted was not unique but, in her case, it was extreme, and will, at least seen from the outside, seem lopsided in someone who had been less

* Plath, *Journals*, 7 July 1958, p.401

** *ibid.*

than sexually abstemious before marriage. Ted did not confront it: 'She cannot be helped that way.'

I do not think Ted had any adulterous affairs before Assia – the affair that began during the visit of Assia and David to Court Green in May 1962, and progressed until she consummated the adultery with Ted about six weeks later. Ted and Sylvia went to Ireland together at the end of the summer, stopping in Wales with Dan and Helga Huws, but the Irish end of the trip was not a success, as Richard Murphy explains in his appendix to *Bitter Fame*. Ted left Court Green at Sylvia's demand just before the point at which – in October and November – the Ariel voice came into fullest force. With an altered emphasis, the voice resumed in the last two weeks of her life, especially with 'Edge', dated 5 February, probably her last poem. In 'Edge' the speaker folds her children into herself and consigns herself and them to oblivion. She had come that far; it was over. It could not have been, as Ted said at first, that she hoped to be saved. The Ariel voice had said what it had to say. 'Daddy, Daddy, you bastard, I'm through,' it said in the first phase, and 'There is nothing between us' and 'Out of the ash / I rise with my red hair / And I eat men like air.' In the second phase it said, 'The heart shuts, / The sea slides back, / The mirrors are sheeted' and 'The woman is perfected.' Ted came to accept this later in part, but, instead of accepting the way she was with other people, he mythologized and thereby transformed his memory of her. *Birthday Letters* recreates the couple as it may have been to themselves, but not as it was to the outside world. Ted needed to mythologize it and Sylvia needed to rationalize it. As it actually happened, Sylvia had completed her work.

Ted cared for the children into adulthood, assisted after a few years by substantial earnings from Sylvia's posthumous publications. If Sylvia had had anything different to say, she would have been someone else and the Ariel voice would have been displaced by a different voice. She would have changed and no longer have been the author of the Ariel poems.

The Ego

Ted was interested in the order of birth. He was a third child, Sylvia and Assia both the first. He tried most of his life to escape the fixed system of the ego; Sylvia did not reckon that other people had egos similar to hers, that the organization of their personalities was based on ego just as hers was, and that the egos of others could not be restricted to supporting her own. What puzzled me most about Ted was that such an extraordinary intellect did not reckon with these contradictions when they applied to Sylvia but did when applied to himself. They facilitated Sylvia's achievement and they also led him into the disasters of his life. Ted only began to work this out in his late fifties and his sixties, and then he sometimes mythologized it. At twenty-three, Sylvia had never had a relationship with a man like the one she developed with Ted. It stood behind the progression of her poetry and also her obsession with death, either of someone else's or, failing that, of herself by suicide. Ted said in 'Flounders' (*Birthday Letters*) that they only did what poetry told them to do. But poetry was telling them different things.

Ted and Sylvia lived in the United States from June 1957 to December 1959 and Ted and I continued, by letter, the exchanges we had begun in Cambridge. He wrote of the attempt to write outside the 'fixed system of the ego' and the 'personal mind'. At Cambridge he stopped writing and did not tell any of his friends he planned to be a poet, although he had not given up that intention. When the Fox visited him in the dream, it told Ted that by 'destroying us', he was destroying his connection to nature and to his creative impulse. He waited to publish, under pseudonyms, until the month of his graduation. When he was living in London, we entered into conversations about escape from the ego and writing objectively. A little more than a year later, he published four poems in the *Saint Botolph's Review*, met Sylvia at the party for its publication, and, in less than four months, married her.

Sylvia encouraged Ted to publish in magazines and typed up his poems. A year after he met her, he won the Harper Prize, judged by Stephen Spender, Marianne Moore and W. H. Auden, for his first group of poems published as *The Hawk in the Rain*. Sylvia had discovered the existence of the contest and prepared his manuscript. In 1960, *Lupercal* came out. These were the two volumes he published when Sylvia was alive. Before escaping from the 'fixed system of the ego' and writing about nature from an objective point of view, he recognized that man is a predatory creature. Many of his poems, like 'Pike', dealt with the predatory system that underlies nature.

Ted himself was unlike this aspect of his poems. He had many friends and, before the complications of marriage and suicide, I heard him express dislike for only one person, the undergraduate who had revealed our names and our roles in giving the young woman a place to sleep in St Botolph's Rectory garden. Ted was from the working class on one side and from the minor entrepreneurial class on the other. His friends were those with whom he shared intellectual concerns. If you put them in a bag and shook them up, some of them would have emerged as unexceptional Cambridge undergraduates and some as gifted. Ted had the unusual capacity of bringing out whatever had been covered over, in most people, by the necessary crust of living with other human beings – of bringing out the peculiarities that make them individual.

The stage after Sylvia's suicide was his confrontation with Crow, a creature unlike the hawk, which was part of nature's design. In 1972, three years after Assia's death and the point at which he could no longer go on with Crow, he bought a farm. Since Carol's father was a farmer and a natural man whom Ted came to care for deeply, a date can be put to the end of this period, the death of Carol's father from cancer in February 1976. Ted's thinking did not change, although it continued to develop, but some other changes had been effected in him. Then the stages run together. He became Poet Laureate in 1984, was increasingly maligned, and finally moved towards the achievement of his last years.

When Ted and Sylvia were married and became convinced that they were complementary beings, he sometimes made remarks in prose that contradicted this. For example, if a poet tried to adapt his style to the taste of a particular editor, he said, he might as well have gone out and got drunk. Yet taking into account an editor's taste was Sylvia's customary procedure, until the poems of the last month carried her beyond such concerns. Her journals show this, time after time, and Ted could only fail to recognize it if he subconsciously ignored it. The practice was not secret and anyone who knew Sylvia knew her concern.

Their concepts of poetry were not the same and so their poetry was not speaking in the same voice. What was spoken in a unified voice was the determination to bring the poetry in them to full expression. Ted thought that poetry possessed a healing characteristic and ignored its other, katabolic characteristic. It has both characteristics since it expresses various human moods. 'Katabolic' was one of Sylvia's favourite words.

Myth, Healing and Predation

Ted did not much like Robert Graves's poetry or novels but *The White Goddess* was not far from his own ideas and foreshadowed their development. On 20 July 1967, he wrote Graves a letter to thank him for being at Poetry International and for writing *The White Goddess*. 'Somebody', Ted said, had given him the book when he was seventeen. The 'somebody' was his inspiring teacher of English at Mexborough Grammar School, who had also written the letter to Pembroke College that helped get him his Cambridge scholarship.

In her book about Sylvia and Ted, Diane Middlebrook uses as bookends Ted's first collected poem, 'Song', and the poem published immediately before his death, 'The Offers'. She presents Sylvia as the White Goddess. Middlebrook's formula is tempting but 'Song' is immature, written at nineteen, and not like the poems he wrote next, beginning at twenty-three. But Sylvia is not the White Goddess. The White Goddess, before she becomes a mother rather than a goddess, represents fertility and not suicide. Sylvia's last poem, 'Edge', is a great poem but its subject is nihilism. The children are folded into the mother. The White Goddess and the relationship between a man and a woman lead to fertility, not nihilism. The batch of poems written in her *annus mirabilis*, late September to mid-November 1962, was neither inspired by nihilism nor by fertility but by resentment.

Ted knew books by foreigners before he knew foreigners. We liked a book called *Specimens of Bushman Folklore* compiled by W. H. I. Bleek with tales on the left-hand side of the page in the Bushman language and the German translations rendered into English on the right.* We liked it partly because the English translation was literal. 'My mother was the one who told me that the girl arose;' it read, 'she

*
W.H.I. Bleek and L.C. Lloyd. *Specimens of Bushman Folklore*. London: George Allen, 1911. The complete text is available online at http://www.archive.org/stream /specimensof-bushm00bleeuo ft/specimensof-bushm00bleeuo ft_djvu.txt

put her hands into the wood ashes; she threw up the wood ashes into the sky. She said to the wood ashes: "The wood ashes which are here, they must altogether become the Milky Way"'. This was a story called 'The Girl Who Made Stars'. There were more than four hundred pages of these stories, all literally translated.

Wilhelm Bleek was born in Berlin in 1827 and died in 1875 on 17 August (Ted's birthday fifty-five years later). Bleek was studying southern African languages when in 1870 the Governor of the Cape Colony agreed to allow Bushman prisoners to be transferred to Bleek's house on the condition that they be locked up at night. This gave Bleek a good opportunity to hear the language, which is full of dental, palatal, cerebral and labial clicks, aspirated gutturals, and croaking sounds. The book did not appear until 1911. We read it in the library. Ted discovered a facsimile copy in a bookshop in London and bought it for me.

Ann Skea, who studied Ted's reflection of the Cabbala, also wrote an essay on his modelling some of his work on vacanas. 'Vacanas', Skea says, 'have no formal metre or rhyme, and very little punctuation. But they do have the "swift, living voice of the oral style" which Ted admired and their rhythms are those of folk-songs, traditional folk-tales and riddles'.* Vacanas had been gathered in a book, *Speaking of Siva*;** they are twelfth-century south Indian poems 'based on the mystical process of becoming one with a god or with a divine Creative Source', as Skea puts it. I did not associate this quest (as according to some scholars, Ted did) with his poem 'Song' – I saw 'Song' as merely a stage in early development.

Ted's thought was unique but elements of his thinking could be found not only in *The White Goddess* but in shamanism and, more explicitly, in the *Bardo Thödol* (Tibetan Book of the Dead). The Bardo lasts forty-nine days (literally or figuratively) and means 'gap or interval between islands or marks', that is, the gap between death and rebirth. *Bardo Thödol* is a guide to the process of dying and death and, unless liberation is achieved, informs the dying of the experiences that he or she will go through in the forty-nine-day passage, all

* See, 'Creatures of Light', paper presented by Ann Skea at Emory University, October 2005.
** Ramanujan, A.K. *Speaking of Siva*. London: Penguin Books, 1973

products of the mind. He can escape them along the way but only the most advanced do and some of these, as Bodhisattvas, return to earthly life to help living beings. The forty-nine-day journey is colourful and terrifying and Ted's description of it is memorable. Ted was working on a libretto for the composer Chou Wen-Chung, whose attraction to the Bardo was different: he told me that its 'colours and images' attracted him. The journey, though, is not a Western way of understanding and therefore not easily transposed into Western music. Six excerpts from Ted's rendering were published in 2006.* The entire translation has not yet been published but is held at Emory University.

Sylvia had some interest in the Bardo. Evans-Wentz, in his introduction to *The Tibetan Book of the Dead*, wrote, '... the Art of Dying is quite as important as the Art of Living (or Coming to Birth), of which it is the complement and summation...'** In October 1962, in 'Lady Lazarus', Sylvia wrote 'Dying / Is an art, like everything else. / I do it exceptionally well.' In 'Fairy Tale' (*Birthday Letters*) Ted wrote, 'Forty-nine was your magic number.' Before she came to England, Sylvia had written a poem called 'Dialogue En Route'. Eve and Adam whirl up through a vertical clockcase, through the forty-ninth floor into space, where thousands were born and dropped dead under a gargantuan galactic wink. It was an entertaining poem and forty-nine was a magic number she continued to invoke. However 'Lady Lazarus' and Evans-Wentz's introduction had nothing in common – they were virtually opposites – except in the use of the number forty-nine.

For Buddhists, the complex of thought has substantive significance, yet Ted was temperamentally more interested in this world than in the world beyond. He was drawn to composition beyond his own consciousness and his own ego – to the claw of the hawk that was the result of the world's evolution – and then called back to things of this world, for example the process of evolution more than why it came about. He was not an anchorite like Buddhist practitioners who used the *Bardo Thödol* to escape the world and approach liberation; he was given to living in the world we are familiar with. He aimed to

* Weissbort, Daniel, ed. *Selected Translations by Ted Hughes.* London: Faber; New York: Farrar, Straus and Giroux, 2006

** Evans-Wentz, W. Y., ed. *The Tibetan Book of the Dead or The After-Death Experiences on the Bardo Plane, according to Lama Kazi Dawa-Samdup's English Rendering.* London: Oxford University Press, 3rd edition, 1957, p.xiii

get beyond the 'personal mind' and escape the fixed system of the ego, but in the end he went back to his fascination with this world. He was the poet who wrote in his libretto for the *Bardo Thödol*, looking down on the kinfolk who mourned the departed, 'They are sweeping out your place.' But, as his thinking evolved, his interest focused on what went on there in that place rather than what went on beyond it. Human beings, it appears, cannot escape their own egos unless they also escape the world.

Shamanism was a more congenial system to Ted's interests than the *Bardo Thödol*. He wrote to me that he had received a 'most marvellous' book to review. He reviewed it and so did I. It was *Shamanism: Archaic Techniques of Ecstasy* by Mircea Eliade, a Romanian scholar at the Ecole des Hautes Etudes in Paris, published in French in 1951 and in English in 1964.* Shamanism functions alongside different religions in many parts of the world, particularly in Central Asia and Central and North America. The shaman is chosen by the spirits and goes through a long and difficult initiation. If the shaman declines election, he or she will sicken or die. The function of the shaman is healing: to accompany a sick person on the journey and bring him or her back to health and a place in the tribe or, failing that, to help the tribe make adjustments to fill the absent one's place.

In using the term 'shamanism' Ted exposed himself to ridicule from critics like Alvarez. As it was, he said we are deaf to this energy today, we are blind to it, and even the most learned are not aware they are actually performing shamanic functions – even the very distinguished, such as T. S. Eliot.* In 1988 the widow of T. S. Eliot assembled his friends at the 'Ecu de France', his favourite London restaurant. Ted gave a toast that described Eliot's shamanic characteristics. Eliot, like modern shamanesque figures, possessed unusual healing powers. It was as though the auto-immune system were at work. He revisits us in his greatest poems and, by them, heals. It is a shamanic function but we do not call it that, since that terminology and function are concealed from us. Poetry, though, has the capacity to heal. Ted, at least, was convinced it had.

---

*
Eliade, Mircea. *Shamanism: Archaic Techniques of Ecstasy*, translated from the French by Willard R. Trask. Princeton, NJ: Princeton University Press, 1970

**
'A Centenary Tribute to T. S Eliot', *Winter Pollen*, London 1994

When Ted first started to publish poems, readers who did not like them commonly disliked them for the 'violence' they found in them. In Yorkshire, Ted had learned that humankind is a predatory creature. Although he had given up hunting in his mid-teens, he fished at every chance he got. The hawk roosting had evolved a beak and a claw; the cathartic bacchanal broke the silence; the salmon was loyal to his doom in the machinery of heaven, which he could not change. Catching a poem was like fishing: you enter into the world of the fish, the wind and water and sky, and you sometimes catch what you came out for. Predation is in the bones of the race and, when it does not come out straightforwardly, it will be expressed indirectly in some variant of fighting – such as scholarly combat or political battle, the disagreements of scholars or political opponents. Predation is part of everyone's nature except for a few anchorites who devote their lives to getting beyond it. As he grew older, poetry took him or he took poetry – in the volume *River* for example – more explicitly into the 'machinery of heaven'.

With my daughter Rosamond, Ted's god-daughter, we went to see friends who lived by the River Dart and Ted got out his waders and fishing tackle. Rosamond went up on the hillside where she would not have to witness fish being caught. It was the only time I saw Ted uncertain of himself. 'I'll throw them back in,' he told her.

*
'A Centenary Tribute to T. S Eliot', *Winter Pollen*, London 1994

Ted and Sylvia

Ted's friends were aware that he did not want them to speak ill of Sylvia and few did for a long time after he died. Sylvia did not speak ill of Ted until they had been married six years, in the second half of 1962 (unless she did so confidentially), but critics subsequently made up for it; some called him a Lothario. The truth was that he invariably had complex relations with people, including women, but he was in no sense a Lothario.

The relationship between Ted and Sylvia had two driving elements: the times and their natures. Sylvia came along at a good time for her adoption as a heroine of the feminist movement. When she died she assumed a place as heroine; not being a feminist herself made her role all the more convincing.

Why was it that only a few first-rate poems preceded the poems from mid-1962 which are the basis of her full reputation? It was because she spoke in the Ariel voice in her late poems but rarely before. It was not for want of trying; it was for want of knowing how to reach the Ariel voice. Instinctively and natively, she knew how to develop technical means and this is particularly clear in her journals, where she is much more often speaking frankly than in her other writings. Her mother encouraged her but only in the fulfilment of her ego, not in the nature of her writing. Others were as gifted and we never hear from them. Sylvia was gifted but Ted was, I think, more gifted. What was exceptional was the interaction between them, which benefited her more than him. Much of his best work was done years after she died. Sylvia realized her gift; Ted realized his only in part.

It was not Ted's adultery that caused the break-up of their marriage, although that was the reason Sylvia presented to her transatlantic correspondents. It was not Assia, displacing her. It was two characteristics within Sylvia herself. One was narcissism, the second was the readiness to say anything which would fit her story, that is, the readiness to say what she wanted others to believe, and her skill in presenting it. The second is a common, human trait; most people deceive themselves for their own benefit from time to time and Sylvia simply did it more effectively than others.

It is, then, the narcissism that is the more exceptional. Sylvia did not compare others to herself because she did not conceive of others as autonomous human beings. She was the world and others were characters in it, not inhabitants of it. Most people think in this way part of the time and also when they are infants; Sylvia could not think in any other way. Ted was the only person who broke through such a disposition, and only to some degree and from time to time.

When Ted had written, in the first introduction to Sylvia's posthumous collection of stories that, 'It seems probable that her real creation was her own image', he was then writing in an analytical but fairly uncharacteristic mode.* It differed from the poetic assessment that began in 1972, evolved until his death in 1998, and was at the heart of *Birthday Letters*. The difference from these was that Ted established a connection with Sylvia that others had not and it resulted in many or most of the poems for which she has become famous. The connection to Sylvia left Ted with an obsession that lasted the rest of his life. Hostile critics projected their own feelings on Sylvia's verse and it was convenient in that process to make Ted a Saint Sebastian.

Ted needed an adverse stimulus just as Sylvia needed a positive one. This fact was seen by no one, not even his friends. When I met Sylvia, I did not realize that he would not be put off by her excesses. I was an American and they struck me forcefully; Ted was an Englishman and they did not strike him in the same way; at the same time, he was in no way inclined to make fun of her, which was the general response. Shirley was a more authentic person but he did not make a comparison. A good part of it was that he liked Sylvia's

* Plath, Sylvia. *Johnny Panic and the Bible of Dreams*. New York: Harper & Row, 1977

excesses. He liked what he took to be her devotion to writing. Possibly, in addition to liking it, he eventually found he had to excuse what went with it. After they reached America, their different perceptions had become very stark, but in their second year he had become more reconciled and she had become more critical. Only her suicide, I thought, disentangled him to some extent.

Ted's belief was self-contradictory, but he was too intelligent not to find a way around it. He had a commonsense view and he was also devoted to poetry. The two are not totally incompatible, but in his case – when it came to Sylvia – he preferred the mythological to the actual. Over twenty-five years, the mythological prevailed over the practical. He began to write *Birthday Letters* in 1972; by the time it had evolved over twenty-five years, its mythology had also evolved. Ted had fully become Otto, her father. She had 'slid' him into Otto. Of course, Ted never met Otto, but he had evolved a view of him. It was a convenient mythology that had some truth to it, but it did not exhaust the truth.

Ted needed Sylvia. He needed her mythology; he loved natural processes, such as he found in farming, he loved people who accepted natural processes, like Jack Orchard, his father-in-law, but he was impatient with ordinary, humdrum life. Sylvia supplied the mythology he needed, in full measure. But what she provided was not based on an interest in anyone but herself, and it applied to no one but herself, though by projection readers were able to substitute themselves for Sylvia. The verse, as well as its merits, had the demerit of ready substitution. It was tempting, even subconsciously, to adopt her voice.

Ted once said that we are full of poems, more than we can ever write, only their full expression was rare. He helped the gift reach its full poetic development in Sylvia, but did not foresee precisely where it would lead them.

Contributors to *Saint Botolph's Review* in 1990, photographed outside the Lamb, Lamb's Conduit Street, London. Left to right, Daniel Huws, David Ross, Daniel Weissbort, Lucas Myers, Ted Hughes.

Acknowledgements

This book was prepared for the conference 'Ted Hughes: From Cambridge to "Collected"' at Pembroke College, Cambridge, September 2010.

We have been grateful for the help of, among others, Carol Hughes, Daniel Huws and Ann Skea.

Extracts from unpublished letters appear by courtesy of the Estate of Ted Hughes.

The main works of Ted Hughes and Sylvia Plath mentioned in the text or cited in the footnotes are:

Hughes, Ted. *Birthday Letters*. London: Faber and Faber, 1998

Hughes, Ted. *Collected Poems*. London: Faber and Faber, 2003

Letters of Ted Hughes. London: Faber and Faber, 2007

The Journals of Sylvia Plath 1950-1962. London: Faber and Faber, 2003

Plath, Sylvia. *Collected Poems*. London: Faber and Faber, 1981

Plath, Sylvia. *Letters Home*. London: Faber and Faber, 1976

Also published
by Richard Hollis and Five Leaves

Ted Hughes and Translation
Daniel Weissbort

—

Memories of Ted Hughes 1952–1963
Daniel Huws

—

Susan Alliston
Poems and Journals 1960–1969
Introduction by Ted Hughes